D0706967

TAKING THE REINS

TAKING THE REINS

Institutional Transformation in Higher Education

Peter D. Eckel
Adrianna Kezar

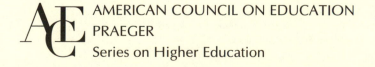
AMERICAN COUNCIL ON EDUCATION
PRAEGER
Series on Higher Education

Library of Congress Cataloging-in-Publication Data

Eckel, Peter D.
   Taking the reins : institutional transformation in higher education / Peter D. Eckel
and Adrianna Kezar.
         p. cm. — (American Council on Education/Praeger Series on Higher
      Education)
   Includes bibliographical references and index.
   ISBN 1–57356–514–8 (alk. paper)
         1. Education, Higher—United States—Administration.   2. Universities and
   colleges—United States—Administration.   3. Educational change—United
   States.   I. Title: Institutional transformation in higher education.   II. Kezar,
   Adrianna J.   III. Title.   IV. Series.
   LB2341.E27   2003
   378.1′01′0973—dc21   2002029881

British Library Cataloguing in Publication Data is available.

Library of Congress Catalog Card Number: 2002029881
ISBN: 1–57356–514–8

First published in 2003

Praeger Publishers, 88 Post Road West, Westport, CT 06881
An imprint of Greenwood Publishing Group, Inc.
www.praeger.com

Printed in the United States of America

The paper used in this book complies with the
Permanent Paper Standard issued by the National
Information Standards Organization (Z39.48–1984).

10 9 8 7 6 5 4 3 2 1

We dedicate this book to those individuals who helped us think more deeply about colleges and universities: Robert Birnbaum, Richard Chait, Madeleine Green, and Anna Neumann. Thank you for encouraging our interest, challenging us to ask difficult questions, and providing us with the tools to seek the answers.

Contents

Preface

Financial pressure, growth in technology, changing faculty roles, public scrutiny, changing demographics, and competition in the world both within and beyond our national borders make change an imperative for higher education. The type of change institutions may have to initiate extends beyond adjustments and growth and accrual, so common in American higher education history, to transformation. Many signs difficult to ignore suggest that more institutions over the next several decades will have to engage in institutional transformation, a type of change different from innovation, adaptation, and strategic change that have been undertaken more frequently in higher education. This book offers insight to campus leaders who face these circumstances to allow them to take charge of major change rather than succumb to environmental challenges. Transformational change is unfamiliar territory for most higher education leaders, uncommon for most institutions, and little discussed in the literature. We attempt to fill that gap.

The purpose of this book is to present a transformational change framework that is theoretically and empirically grounded and rich in context. The material comes from working with and observing twenty-three diverse institutions as they sought to effect various types of institutional change and transformation through a longitudinal American Council on Education (ACE) project seeking to understand better the process of institutional transformation. This project, funded by the W. K. Kellogg Foundation, provided us access to the range of experiences and approaches used by institutions seeking to make meaningful academic change. Through research conducted as part of this project, we developed what we present here as the Mobile Model of change. Over the course of the book, we present the key aspects of the model—including core change strategies, the interrelationship among strategies, the role of "sensemaking," and the need for attention to institutional culture. At the book's conclusion, we put all the pieces together into a coherent model.

The impetus for the book and its organization grew out of a series of presentations and discussions that we had at national meetings of higher education researchers and campus leaders. It seemed that each time we presented a portion of the research, the discussion inevitably turned to a portion of work presented elsewhere. People with whom we interacted sought the whole picture of institutional transformation, not just the piece we were discussing at that moment. This book allows us to put together the pieces into a coherent whole that a series of journal articles and presentations did not.

We based this book on the belief that institutional leaders and policy makers have neither the experience with institutional transformation nor a solid empirical literature base on which to draw. There is little meaningful data to advance an understanding of the *process* of large-scale or transformational change (although notable exceptions do exist, including Lindquist, 1978; Sporn, 1999). The literature on change in higher education does not focus on transformation as a specific type of change. Even when scholarship focuses on change as a broader topic, it is informative about the content of change (see, for example, St. John, 1991; Gumport, 1993), what factors are related to the change outcomes (see El-Khawas, 1995), and the conditions related to change (see Hearn, 1996), but not the processes leaders must use to bring about change, let alone transformation.

Within the literature on the process of change in higher education is a lack of empirical data. Sometimes the strategies offered in the literature are grounded in research (see, for example, Leslie & Fretwell, 1996), but predominantly, they are reflections of former college leaders, which, although informative, tend not to be grounded in research outside their immediate experiences. Second, change strategies tend to be generalizations, such as a willing president or strong leadership, a motivating vision and mission, or aligning values and policies. Suggestions such as "involve the faculty" and "improve communication" provide little practical advice to leaders faced with implementing deep and pervasive change. A third issue is that much of the literature presents change strategies as isolated, distinct actions and does not offer strategies for institution-wide change as systemic, concurrent, and interdependent. Management author Henry

Mintzberg notes, "Organizational strategies cannot be created by the logic used to assemble automobiles" (1994, p. 13). Viewing organizational processes systemically is essential to improving administration and gaining a better understanding of the ways institutions function. It also more accurately reflects the realities of institutional life, in all its complexities and jumble. Using theoretical or conceptual frameworks that illustrate the dynamism within and among organizational phenomena is extremely powerful.

Some of the research in higher education suggests that institutional transformation is unlikely unless the institution is faced with an overwhelming external crisis, such as undergoing extreme financial problems or being mandated by state or system policy. We do not agree. We do subscribe to the belief, however, that many, if not most, institutions that engage institutional transformation are already in a state of flux resulting from a combination of external pressure and emerging opportunities. Savvy leaders know when to take advantage of externally generated energy and match it to internal desires and goals. Transformation may not be as much about an institution off-balance; instead, engaging in these strategies can add a sense of direction and purpose and thus create stability.

We acknowledge that institutional transformation is difficult and that institutions must carefully decide whether to engage in institutional transformation because it is a precarious process that can create upheaval and ill feelings throughout the institution. When institutional leaders (both faculty and administrators) can take the reins of change, they and the institutions they serve are in much better positions to fulfill the important social roles colleges and universities must play in a future highly driven by information and knowledge.

The audience for this book is intended to be quite broad. The main audience consists of members of colleges and universities who have the responsibility for leading change or who are interested in understanding better how transformation occurs in academe. Institutional leaders, such as presidents and provosts, deans and department chairs, senate heads, and faculty committee chairs, as well as other campus administrators, should find this book a helpful resource because it focuses on the processes of change. It may complement other books and resources that focus on a particular change, such as institutionalizing posttenure review or developing student outcomes assessment strategies, for example, that give short shrift to implementation processes. Readers will learn about transformation processes and be introduced to a language of transformation that will help them to facilitate the institution-wide change processes on their campuses. For many, the findings will simply reinforce beliefs and hunches developed from their experiences; for others, it will present new ideas or different ways of thinking. Trustees and policy makers may also benefit from the information synthesized and analyzed in this book to gain a better understanding of large-scale academic change.

Higher education scholars are another intended audience for this book. Recent years have seen a renewed interest in change and transformation, and more researchers are beginning to focus on this area. Increasingly, programs in higher education administration programs have developed new courses on change or courses on leadership in which change is a major component. The growing number of classes in this area might adopt this text.

A final audience for the book is higher education leadership development programs that incorporate modules on change management. Numerous national associations, state systems, and others have developed programs on higher education leadership and management. We expect it will be difficult to develop a program intended to shape future academic leaders without including components on leading change and transformation. The importance of these topics should only grow as institutions and their environments become more complex.

This book is organized into seven chapters. The first chapter provides the context for transformation in American higher education. It explores the challenges colleges and universities face, including those created by technology, globalization, competition and the marketplace, student demographics, and new financial realities. It defines the concept of transformation as we use it here, provides a glimpse of our proposed model for transformation, and describes the ACE project on which this book is based. The second chapter delves more deeply into the concept of transformation, particularly its depth and pervasiveness, and the ways it affects institutional cultures. This chapter also explores transformation by setting it against other types of change common to colleges and universities including innovation, adaptation, and strategic change. It concludes by providing a template to determine the extent of change on a campus.

Chapter 3 begins our discussion of the components of our model of transformation. It focuses on one of the essential activities of transformation, institutional sensemaking. The reader learns that more important to transformation than changing structures, creating incentives, and aligning budgets is getting people to think differently. This chapter explores the notion of institutional sensemaking as it applies to transformation and identifies key activities that support this process by drawing on the experiences of those institutions making the most progress toward transformation.

Chapter 4 introduces the five core strategies that we identify as essential to transformation—senior administrative support, collaborative leadership, flexible vision, staff development, and visible action. It describes each strategy and provides rich examples of the ways that they have played themselves out at different institutions. Chapter 5 describes additional, supporting strategies important to effecting transformational change. We describe these strategies and provide illustrations. We also demonstrate the ways in which the core and supporting strategies work in concert with one another and are interdependent. The final purpose of Chapter 5 is to describe the importance of balance throughout the long and complicated transformational change process.

Chapter 6 explores the ways in which institutional culture shapes the change process. Although transformation will alter institutional cultures in some ways, those cultures also shape the change process. Understanding one's own culture is important to creating effective transformation processes.

The final chapter pulls together the various elements essential to transformational change. We summarize the key points from the earlier chapters and demonstrate the ways in which they work together to promote transformation. We use the metaphor of a mobile to illustrate the ways in which the core and supporting strategies are interrelated, the role of sensemaking in pulling the pieces together, the importance of balance, and the effect of culture on the process of transformation. This model helps organize the complexity of our findings and can serve as a useful tool and heuristic devise as institutional leaders work to advance major change on campus.

Acknowledgments

Just as institutional transformation is a complex undertaking that requires hard work, good ideas, interest, and commitment from many people, so did writing this book. We first want to acknowledge the dedication and commitment of the institutions and their leaders participating in the ACE Project on Leadership and Institutional Transformation. Their almost six years of on-campus effort and participation in the project made this work possible. We appreciate the openness and candor of faculty and administrative leaders who shared their thoughts, challenges, successes, and failures with us and with each other. Getting to know intimately institutions and the people who work in them provided the foundation on which this book is built. We are constantly in awe of the dedication, thoughtfulness, and passion of those with whom we worked and observed. We appreciate getting to know them as higher education leaders and as colleagues. For this and more that is not easily articulated, we say thank you.

We acknowledge the generosity and encouragement of the W. K. Kellogg Foundation and our program officers, Betty Overton, who supported the ACE Project on Leadership and Institutional Transformation, and John Burkhardt, who supported the subsequent project, the Kellogg Forum on Higher Education Transformation (KFHET). Without their steadfast support and encouragement, we might not have had the passion and resolve to continue this effort over time. It is atypical for foundations to support efforts more than five years, and we appreciate the hope they inspired by allowing us to do things a bit differently. We hope that they are as pleased with the results of their investment as we are.

We acknowledge the ACE staff and the consultants whose thinking, noodling, questioning, and challenging helped shape the ideas presented here. We put the words to paper, but the ideas would not have been as clear and coherent without the hours of discussion and thinking that supported our work. We acknowledge the importance of the On Change occasional paper series that many had a hand in writing and shaping as the precursor to this book. We thank the project consultants and ACE staff who visited campuses, facilitated focus groups, and contributed ideas throughout the project: Mary-Linda Amacost, Narcisa Polonio, Patricia Plante, Donna Shavlik, Bob Shoenberg, and Deb Wilds. Barbara Hill, a consultant to ACE, contributed not only to the visits and meetings but also to the conceptual work of the project and to many of the ideas that appear in these pages. She served as the lead author of the On Change paper written for trustees regarding institutional transformation. Her intellect made us better thinkers. We acknowledge the contributions of Colleen Allen, who helped manage the project and keep both it and us on track. We appreciate the assistance and advice provided by ACE's Jim Murray and Wendy Bresler to turn these ideas into a book. Thanks also to Carol Corneilse at the University of Maryland, who helped us polish the manuscript and get our references in order.

We reserve the final thanks for Madeleine Green, vice president at ACE and project director. Without her leadership, encouragement, support, and willingness to raise and address tough questions, we would not have written this book or had these insights. We appreciate her ability to find clarity in the ambiguities of institutional transformation and her thoughtfulness to make it all meaningful to campus leaders.

CHAPTER 1

The Context for Transformation

Higher education is a dynamic enterprise. It is continually evolving, although with a good deal of struggle and challenge, to better prepare its students, generate new knowledge, and address society's most-pressing problems. Change, as well as continuity, is part of the academy. One cannot pick up the *Chronicle of Higher Education*, any disciplinary association's publications, *Change* magazine, or for that matter, the *New York Times* or *USA Today* without seeing stories about innovative pedagogies in a range of disciplines, cutting-edge scholarship, distance education that expands access and generates new tuition dollars, new applications of technology, or institutions marshaling their resources to improve their local communities. However, one also sees headlines about cutbacks in state funding and endowment returns, nontraditional for-profit institutions granting degrees, abysmal graduation rates of Division I athletes, inequities in the graduation of majority and minority students, attacks on affirmative action in the courts, and intrusive governing boards and public officials. To paraphrase a well-known writer, for many institutions it is both the best of times and the worst of times. Administrators and faculty leaders are working hard at ensuring their institutions are successful in this new century.

Much of what colleges and universities should do remains consistent with their historic purposes and roles. Society, tuition-paying students and their families, employers, and elected officials expect colleges and universities to fulfill important social roles. Colleges and universities prepare eighteen- to twenty-two-year-olds to be productive citizens for the world of work or advanced degrees; they provide adult students with new skills and knowledge to meet their changing personal and professional goals; they are expected to be important engines for local economic development; and they conduct research and provide disinterested commentary to address social issues. In many instances, colleges and universities will change not to do new things but to do what they historically have done, only better.

This book is about making those necessary broad changes, about improving institutions to fulfill their public responsibilities in an ever-changing society. It discusses a particular type of change—transformation—that some institutions will undertake as they work toward meeting their social and educational objectives in an environment in which the rules are continually being rewritten, and it proposes a set of strategies that institutions can use to bring about transformation.

NEW TIMES, NEW CHALLENGES

Institutions vary tremendously. They serve different populations of students, are located in different geographic contexts, and have their own histories and cultures. Yet they face many similar circumstances and challenges: attending to budget shortfalls, seeking to improve student learning, and trying to create a unique identity for themselves. The following scenarios reflect the challenges three of the institutions in the ACE Project on Leadership and Institutional Transformation faced that led them on the journey of transformation.[1]

Midwest College

The week prior to the start of classes, a newly elected president of Midwest College, a liberal arts college, assembled a special daylong retreat to issue a challenge to the faculty: "Given the choices, why should a student choose this college?"

That morning's retreat began with a discussion of the college's current situation: An overview of the operating budget of $35 million and a report on its $13 million endowment. The faculty learned that 85 percent of all revenues came from tuition and that, in fact, enrollments had been in a steady decline for the past five years. That year's enrollment of 790 students was the lowest in twelve years. The financial woes were compounded by a racial incident two years earlier that caught national attention and caused African-American students to leave in droves after a brawl in the residence halls between an African-American student and two white students. The president publicly surmised at the morning retreat that after one bad year, he might have to "sell the buildings and turn off the lights." The picture he painted, although bleak, he thought was not too outlandish.

That challenge and the retreat started a series of events that led the college to embark on major change—a transformation that resulted in a new institutional mission driven by a widely agreed upon set of values, one that altered the culture of the institution and that created deep and widespread changes in how the college operates, its priorities, curriculum, and pedagogies, as well as its expectations for students and faculty—one that ultimately resulted in more students, ones serious about obtaining a higher education and who believed in the institution's values.

Middle State University

In the mid-1980s, the president of Middle State University, a one-time teacher's college and now a regional doctoral-granting university, secured a commitment from the state to fund a set of technological enhancements for the campus. This influx of funds allowed the university to purchase computers for every faculty member at a time when computers were still a luxury at many similar institutions. The university, over time, has created a campuswide technological infrastructure to support high-end computing across campus. For example, all classrooms are wired for internal communications, more than forty computer labs are available for students twenty-four hours a day, and more than one hundred classrooms allow the use of multiple technologies. More than $300,000 is awarded annually to faculty to support teaching innovation using technology. Along with this infrastructure, campus leaders—faculty, department chairs, and senior administrators—have developed a widely shared ethos of technological sophistication that has infused the campus, reshaping the student experience as well as the classroom.

While this technological boom was occurring, the institution struggled to find its place and identity within the state between two research universities and a set of open-admission colleges. Deciding that quality teaching, along with technology, would be its badge of honor, faculty leaders initiated a campuswide conversation about the importance of teaching to expand their university's definition of scholarship to include teaching as facilitated by technology. Over the next decade, the university positioned itself within the state as the high-tech university of choice for undergraduate students, striving to become a selective residential public institution. It engaged in widespread curricular and academic program innovations, it saw the quality of its student body rise, it increased the size of its honors program, and it tripled the number of National Merit scholars. Faculty on campus no longer believe themselves to be working at a second-tier institution. They talk about their university as a leader in higher education and see that role as defined by their technological sophistication and focus on undergraduate learning. This new sense of self permeates the university and positively affects the student experience. Students are now proud to attend a university that many once thought of as a place of last resort. They sense a high-quality education and can articulate the ways in which a technologically intense experience has prepared them well.

Sunshine Community College

Although Sunshine Community College was seeing a steady growth in its enrollments, was opening a new campus, and was viewed well by the local business community, the faculty and administrative leaders of this southern college were uncomfortable. They believed the college was falling short in its primary focus of student learning. A group of faculty and administrators wondered if the college had been focusing too much on "teaching," instead of placing "learning" at the center of its activities. They also questioned whether the ideas of teaching and learning were fundamentally different. They wondered what it would mean for the college to focus on the outcomes of the teaching rather than on the activity of teaching itself. They recognized that their current, guiding assumption was that if teaching was supported, learning would naturally occur. They began to speculate about what would happen if the college became learning centered, rather than faculty or teaching centered.

Asking these questions led faculty and administrators to develop a campuswide process, heavily based on continual and widespread conversation and joint decision making that examined the ways in which the college's teaching-centered assumptions influenced its activities, structures, decisions, priorities, and procedures. The result of their concerted efforts over five years was the recognition and adoption of four core learning competencies—Think, Value, Communicate, Act—that in turn reshaped the institution's general education program, guided curricular change within a set of majors, created a new student advising infrastructure, framed a Title III grant, and created an extensive faculty development program. The process changed the way in which the college talked about itself, and conversations about learning came to dominate standing meetings as well as hallway conversations. The ideas of learning, rather than of teaching, became woven into the fabric of the college.

The Challenge

Although these three institutions are of different types, and they are working on a variety of change agendas, the common denominator of their experience is that each has made significant progress toward transforming itself. Change for these institutions is not an isolated phenomenon, nor is it a one-time event; and it is not an innovation or an adaptation. These colleges and universities are in the process of changing their cultures; they have developed new processes, structures, offices, and priorities; they have made consistent and reinforcing changes to their curricula, pedagogies, reward structures, and budgets; and they recognize that their work continues. The language these institutions use to talk about themselves, about their students, and about their common purposes is distinctively different from what it was before they undertook their efforts. The ways in which faculty interact with students are different, as are the ways in which administrators and faculty work together to accomplish institutional tasks and meet newly recognized responsibilities. Widespread and frequent campus conversations reflect a new sense of being and a new institutional identity. These institutions set out to intentionally make deep and lasting widespread change, and they are doing so.

How did these institutions and others like them implement widespread and transformational change? What strategies did they use? Much common wisdom about change in higher education suggests that institutional leaders (1) develop a plan, possibly a strategic plan with a set of steps, to reshape the direction and activities of their campus (such as identified by their strengths, weaknesses, opportunities, and threats); (2) reexamine faculty roles and rewards, carefully modify reward structures and added incentives, and implement new promotion and tenure guidelines to overcome faculty resistance or indifference; and (3) follow the decisive vision of senior administrators who set the direction into the uncharted future.

Common wisdom carries some truth, but after almost six years of working with, and learning from, a diverse set of institutions seeking to implement transformational change, we saw other things more important at institutions progressing on the institution-wide change agendas that challenged common wisdom. We learned that although leadership from senior administrators is important, alone it is insufficient. For some institutions, a strategic plan played an important role, but for others, it was nonexistent. Not one institution started with changing reward structures or intentionally sought to modify promotion and tenure policies as a lever of change, although over time, these policies and practices evolved to match emerging new institutional priorities.

We write this book to share the insights gleaned from institutions undertaking institutional change. The purpose of this book is to offer a competing set of notions to much of the common wisdom about effecting change in colleges and universities. In these pages, we explore the ways in which the above three institutions and others like them have gone about what we call *institutional transformation*. Based on a national project involving twenty-three diverse institutions over a six-year period, this book is about taking the reins of change, about charting an institution's own course in the dynamic environment that higher education finds itself. It presents our concept of transformation, identifies key elements essential to bringing about desired comprehensive change, and places these elements into a model based on empirical research.

THE CHANGING ENVIRONMENT FOR HIGHER EDUCATION

The foregoing scenarios represent the realities facing many American colleges and universities. Improving and assessing student learning, finding ways to capitalize on new technology, making difficult decisions regarding allocating scarce resources, admitting and educating a changing cohort of students, developing ways to distinguish oneself from other institutions, and finding new and better ways to meet the needs of the local community and society at large are just some of the challenges that American institutions face. As the changing environment pushes institutions to do new things, many faculty, staff, and administrators strive to improve their institutions, enhancing much of what they already do well. The circumstances in which the three institutions described in the preceding section find themselves are more likely familiar than not.

The pressures for change have been well documented by others (for example, see Frank Newman's working papers from the Futures Project at www.futuresproject.org/) and are readily recalled without much prompting; thus, they require only a summary discussion in this book. Reports and essays, as well as accounts in both the popular and education media, detail these changes extensively, including the following: the effect of the digital revolution on higher education, the new financial environment in which both public and private institutions find themselves, changing demographics that bring more older and more racially and ethnically diverse students to our doorsteps (for instance, called Tidal Wave II in California because of its predicted magnitude), the rise of competition for students, faculty, and fiscal resources that generate new strategies and programs, and the demands of globalization and internationalization that push institutions to look beyond their geographic borders.

The following sections briefly outline some of the more significant well-known and keenly articulated pressures pushing higher education to do new things, to reconsider its ways of working and its priorities, and to chart new social missions.

Technology

Ask anyone what the largest pressure for change has been over the past five to seven years, and they are likely to respond, "technology." Technology has entered the classrooms, shaping pedagogies, changing lectures, and (we hope) enhancing learning. Some predict that as technology gains an increasingly sure foothold, it will make traditional modes of teaching and learning less and less practical (Newman & Scurry, 2001). For some, this technologically enriched future is desirable because higher education will benefit (Obligner, Barone, and Hawkins, 2001; Twigg, 1999); for others, it is not so welcomed (Kriger, 2001). And for still others, it is described as solely inevitable and neutral, it being up to higher education to take up the challenge of quality, fit, and purpose (Duderstadt, 2000; Katz, 1999).

New ways to package, explain, and deliver information, as well as new pathways to communicate between instructor and student and among students, are presenting new opportunities and new challenges. However, in many instances, technology is simply a new bottle for an old wine. When technology is used only to post syllabi or lecture notes, or becomes simply a substitute for a telephone, it does not have much potential to transform teaching and learning. When technology changes the requisite distance between professor and students or removes dependence on time from their interactions, when it creates opportunities for active learning, such as through the immediate application of knowledge, provides instantaneous feedback, or allows for costly scientific experiments to be performed by large numbers of students, it can have transformational effects.

However, most discussions of technology in the academy focus on classroom application. Beyond the classroom, it can be profoundly catalytic for institutional change. For example, technology can be used to tremendously expand access to higher education. Technology has provided the fundamental building block for efforts such as the Kentucky Virtual University and the African Virtual University. In the United States, more than two thousand institutions offer on-line courses; enrollment more than doubled between 1994–95 and 1997–98 to 1,632,350 (Newman & Couturier, 2001). On-line enrollment at places such as the University of Maryland University College and Pennsylvania State University's World Campus is reported to have grown in two years by 1,000 percent and 200 percent, respectively (PricewaterhouseCoopers and the University of North Carolina, as cited in Obligner, Barone, & Hawkins, 2001). This growth in enrollment brings different types of students into the academy. In addition to providing access to students who are unable to attend traditional classroom-based education (such as students in rural America), on-line courses allow many adult students to gain access. Traditional higher education is anticipated to grow by an additional 2.6 million students by 2015, and 31 percent of those new students will be adults, working full-time, with family responsibilities (Carnevale & Fry, 2001).

Beyond having the potential to reshape the classroom and extend access, technology is raising new administrative and governance challenges. Technology is fostering new partnerships with for-profit providers and technology hardware and software companies to deliver distributed or distance education. For example, UNext is partnering with Carnegie Mellon University, the London School of Economics and Political Science, and the University of Chicago, among others, to develop and market technology-rich courses to corporate clients. Technology becomes the catalyst between institutions in the United States and abroad to offer new joint academic programs. The Global University Alliance is a revenue-generating partnership between George Washington University and the University of Wisconsin-Milwaukee in the United States and universities in Canada, the United Kingdom, Australia, and Europe that offers courses and degrees on-line. Because many of these efforts have curriculum and learning at their core, they raise new challenges for traditional academic decision making. How do institutions make decisions about new academic programs and approve new courses when they are offered off-campus to new student populations, when multiple institutions are involved, when there is an oversight body, and when revenue is generated and must be shared? Because the decision to participate in new technology-driven partnerships involving teaching and learning is both strategic and curricular, who has primary oversight, the board or the faculty senate? Technology is, in many instances, blurring an already fuzzy line.

New Financial Environment

The financial context within which most public and private universities must work continues to change, and in most cases it is becoming more constraining. Public allocations are not keeping pace with expenses, federal research dollars are fluctuating, foundations are turning away from higher education or becoming more selective in their funding, and the tuition-paying public will likely believe costs are too high and will not stand for tuition increases to make up budgetary shortfalls (Hovey, 1999; Ikenberry & Hartle, 2000; Morino Institute, 2001). Even in times of growing economies, institutions have not seen a proportional increase in their allocations. Instead, they are relying more heavily on endowment returns and gifts and are engaging in cost-cutting measures or entrepreneurial activities to create opportunities elsewhere (Clark, 1998; Marginson & Considine, 2000). Diversifying the resource base seems to be the preferred strategy of the moment; the realities of additional public funding are slim at best. The new fiscal realities are not limited to the United States, as countries worldwide, some with long histories of strong state support, are looking to tap new sources of income (Green & Hayward, 1997).

At the same time, higher education costs are rising as a result of increased administrative costs, more outlays for student services and scholarships, and higher instructional expenditures for library books and journals, research equipment, computers, and other educational necessities. The fiscal realities push higher education to find solutions that simultaneously reduce academic costs and create new academic programs, support an ever-growing and expensive technology infrastructure, keep faculty salaries competitive, and maintain an expensive, and in some instances neglected, physical plant.

In an effort to live within new financial constraints, many institutions have become much more savvy in auxiliary services. Examples include licensing arrangements and patents, purchasing and procurement, physical plant maintenance, and capital improvement, as well as streamlined accounting procedures. Many institutions are forming public-private partnerships to build and run residence halls and entering agreements with state and local governments to support projects that benefit both the university and local communities. For instance, the University of Maryland, in conjunction with the state of Maryland and Prince George's County, as well as private donors, opened The Clarice Smith Performing Arts Center, a $130 million, seventeen-acre, 318,000-square-foot performing arts center, one of the largest facilities of its kind on any university campus in the country.

The current fiscal realities also push institutions into a variety of entrepreneurial activities, some of which relate directly to the academic mission of the institution, others not as much, although their proponents attempt to make a compelling case. For instance, universities have become real estate developers, creating and maintaining technology parks that bring in dollars and facilitate partnerships between their academic departments and their corporate tenants. Some institutions are offering certificates and nondegree short courses, either in local markets or on contract from area corporations and local government. Research universities, in particular, are developing and capitalizing on research and expertise to tap new sources of income. Some suggest that these activities mirror the realities of nonprofit life today (Clark, 1998); others suggest that this represents the corporate takeover of higher education that will cause irreparable harm (White & Hauck, 2000).

New Markets and Competition

Higher education is becoming an increasingly competitive arena. No longer is competition relegated to the playing fields of intercollegiate athletics. All colleges and universities compete for students, financial resources, faculty, and possibly most important, reputation. As the fiscal environment becomes less abundant and inadequate, institutions will have to supplement their state allocations and returns on endowments with revenue-generating activities in the marketplace. Focusing on new student populations and the tuition dollars they bring in is a primary strategy. Institutions are developing graduate and weekend programs to tap into the adult student market. When employers are footing the bill, degree- and certificate-granting, as well as noncredential, programs can be especially lucrative. Simply look at the rise of executive management programs. Colleges and universities are also developing approaches to entice the best students, who, in many cases, are able to shoulder a higher burden of the cost of their education. State schools are competing with merit-based financial aid, and private institutions are shifting their institutional-aid policies to recruit better students, leaving behind the students most in need of financial aid, the less qualified and less affluent (Newman & Scurry, 2001). However, as competition for students grows, so does their ability to influence institutional priorities. Students who are not satisfied with their educational experience can vote with their feet, taking with them their prized tuition and fees.

The competitive arena for students does not start and stop with traditional degree-granting two- and four-year institutions. New for-profit providers, corporate universities, and certificate programs are emerging as tempting alternatives for students. The University of Phoenix, a for-profit, regionally accredited institution, as of 2000 operated fifty-five campuses and ninety-eight learning centers, offers courses on-line, and serves eighty-four thousand students (Kriger, 2001). It is still growing. The Education Commission of the States (ECS) identified more than 660 for-profit institutions operating in the United States as of 1999 (Brimah, 2000). It is safe to speculate that this sector is most likely growing, although the e-learning dot-coms are going through a shakeout similar to their Wall Street kin. The competitors also include institutions and organizations that are unlike traditional degree-granting institutions, even for-profit, accredited universities. Approximately 1.6 million individuals worldwide earned around 2.4 million certificates in information technology by early 2000 (Adelman, 2000). Roughly two thousand "corporate universities" now exist, offering training and development programs to their own employees and to those from other firms (Meister, 2001). Most of these corporate university and information technology (IT) certification students and their education fall outside of higher education's accreditation, quality assurance, and credit structures, into what Adelman (2000) calls a "parallel universe." In some instances, they are simply expanding the number of students involved in postsecondary education; in others, they are competing with traditional institutions for students and faculty. The e-learning world is anticipated to generate revenues of more than $1 billion in 2005 (Newman, Chen, & Gallagher, 2002).

Changing Student Demographics

American higher education has long known about the approaching changing demographics of students entering its campuses. No longer can colleges and universities await the multicultural future; it is here. Students from diverse social, ethnic, and racial backgrounds constitute a growing proportion of the population as a whole and are increasingly seeking a higher education. The numbers of African-American, Asian-American, and Hispanic students completing high school continue to climb. Among Hispanic students, that number has almost tripled in the last twenty years (Harvey, 2001). States such as Texas, New York, and Florida will continue to witness tremendous population growth in both numbers and diversity. The Educational Testing Service (ETS) predicts that more than 80 percent, or 2 million, of the projected 2.6 million new undergraduate students enrolled by 2015 will be students of color. In three states—Hawaii, California, and New Mexico—and the District of Columbia, more "minority" students will be enrolled than white students by that time (Carnevale & Fry, 2001). Although the racial and ethnic changes will the greatest in ten states (Hodgkinson, 1999), diversity remains an important educational issue across the nation.

However, as the racial and ethnic composition of our campuses continues to diversify, the success of most of these students remains far behind their white contemporaries. For example, according to the 2000 census, 16 percent of all Hispanics and 21 percent of all African Americans over the age of 25 had earned a college degree, compared with 35 percent of whites and 49 percent of Asian Americans. The six-year graduation rate at Division I colleges and universities for Hispanic students remained unchanged between 1992 and 1997 at 45 percent, which trails both whites (58 percent in 1997) and Asian Americans (65 percent in 1997); for African Americans, the graduation rate is 40 percent, unchanged between 1993 and 1998 (Harvey, 2001). The same data note the graduation rate for African American males is 31 percent. African Americans received just 8.3 percent of all bachelor's degrees; however, they represent 11 percent of all undergraduate enrollments. And Hispanic students earned 5.6 percent of all bachelors' degrees, even though they were 9 percent of the total enrollment (Harvey, 2001).

Furthermore, the average age of undergraduates continues to change as more adult students seek advanced education. When age diversity is combined with racial and ethnic diversity, one can see that American higher education is serving a different type of student than it did previously. For instance, the majority of African-American students currently enrolled are women over the age of twenty-four who have dependents (King, 1999). The typical student is no longer an eighteen to twenty-two-year-old white residential undergraduate. In fact, American higher education may no longer have a "typical student," and the numbers suggest that higher education is not adequately ensuring the success of all students. Without meeting this challenge, U.S. higher education risks contributing to continued inequities and undermining its democratic principles.

Globalization

All of these trends are occurring at a time marked by globalization, when the world is metaphorically getting smaller and much, if not most, contemporary knowledge has an international dimension. Economies can no longer be defined as simply domestic, arts and science transcend cultures, and countries that select isolationist policies pay for it in political mistakes, ignorance of new developments in science and health care, and economic stagnation (Duderstadt, 2000; Green & Hayward, 1997). Institutions strive to promote international competence in their graduates, and many have images that reflect these global trends proudly displayed in their undergraduate recruitment materials.

However, American higher education has paid scant attention to internationalization beyond foreign language and area studies, where it tends to be relegated. Federal funding for international education in the United States remains a low priority, even though former president Bill Clinton, in one of his final acts, attempted to focus national attention on international education by issuing a presidential memorandum on international education policy. Less than 3 percent of all undergraduates study abroad, language course enrollment continues to skid from a high of 16 percent in the 1960s to less than 8 percent today, and federal funding to support internationalizing undergraduate education has declined over the past decade (Hayward, 2000). As the former president of a major public research university wrote:

American knowledge of other languages and cultures is abysmally inadequate. Too many of our graduates have never been exposed to a foreign language or visited a foreign country. Many have not had a chance to feel the texture of life in another era or another culture through literature and poetry or film. By every measure we fall short educationally of the knowledge and skills it will take to do business, to work cooperatively on common problems, or to advance our common ideals for humanity. (Duderstadt, 2000, pp. 18–19)

In contrast, European countries, as well as the supranational European Union, are giving internationalization a high priority by providing programs, incentives, and funding to promote the international exchange of students and faculty, by supporting collaborative programs and research efforts that cross national borders, and by encouraging a broadening of the curriculum to include international issues.

Many American colleges and universities have extensive international linkages, large cadres of international scholars and students (particularly graduate students), and diverse curricula that include literature and history from abroad, making it difficult to say that U.S. colleges and universities are not international. Nevertheless, internationalization on most campuses is limited to the experiences of a few students who study abroad or major in area studies or languages, or it occurs because of serendipity rather than intentionally. Most students tend to bump into internationalization rather than be intentionally steered toward it. Rarely does internationalization reach deeply into the curriculum or become a substantial and meaningful component of an undergraduate student's education.

The Interaction Effects

Higher education has faced a history of challenges, and it would be short-sighted to suggest that today's challenges are greater than yesterday's ones (Birnbaum, 2000; Eccles & Norhia, 1992). However, as the environment continues to change, the above challenges will commingle, interact, and bump into one another, leading to a newfound complexity and creating new complicated territory for institutional leaders to tread that most likely will not be served by piecemeal changes.

Technology, Competition, and Globalization

Technology, competition, and globalization are combining in many ways to create new challenges for university leaders. Technology allows universities and other educational providers to extend their reach abroad, intensifying competition, and often crossing borders. The University of Phoenix has campuses and learning centers in multiple states and reaches students elsewhere through distance education. Transnational partnerships, such as the Global University Alliance, a collaboration between Athabasca University (Canada), The Auckland University of Technology, The George Washington University, the International Business School (Hogeschool Brabant) in the Netherlands, the Royal Melbourne Institute of Technology, the University of Derby (United Kingdom), University of Glamorgan (Wales), University of South Australia, and the University of Wisconsin-Milwaukee, offer a range of the on-line courses and programs from each partner to a wider number of students in a broader set of countries. The ministers of education of twenty-nine European countries signed the Bologna Declaration in June 1999, which has as one of its primary objectives to increase the "competitiveness and attractiveness" of European higher education, increasing the presence of European universities in the global postsecondary market. Global competition is not limited to traditional universities. For example, during the last six months of 2000, Cisco certification and training courses took place in nineteen different languages, including Czech, Dutch, Finnish, German, Polish, Russian, and Turkish, and are offered on every inhabited continent (Adelman, 2000).

Another potential outcome of the intersection of these trends is the rise of globally recognized "name-brand" universities that come to dominate markets worldwide because of their prestige. For example, the business schools at Harvard and Stanford universities are jointly creating an executive management program. Across borders, the Wharton School of Business at the University of Pennsylvania formed an alliance with France's INSEAD. Independently, each institution from these examples is a powerful brand name. Together, they hope to create an even more attractive alliance. The potential threat is that alliances between widely recognized institutions would offer programs that relegate other institutions to less-prosperous market segments. However, the reality of a future higher education dominated by a few global brand-name institutions is still distant (Green, Eckel, & Barblan, 2002).

What the intersection of these trends means for higher education is unclear. Nevertheless, higher education leaders can no longer simply keep an eye on local markets, create strategies that are tied only to surrounding needs, or merely benefit from opportunities in one's backyard. Competition, globalization, and technology create new, complicated challenges, as well as nebulous opportunities.

Student Demographics and Competition

The changing student demographics coupled with a rise in competition can create difficult circumstances and lead to tough choices for institutions. The new students, who mostly will come from underrepresented populations, call for different and expanded academic programs, enhanced and additional student services, and changes in structures and operating procedures, such as expanded office hours and adequate and flexible child care for working adult students. However, as competition becomes more intense, the needs of these students at many institutions may well take a back seat to other priorities, such as recruiting highly talented students or faculty or developing programs that support niche-market activities. An increasingly intense academic free market presents certain choices to campus leaders to bolster institutional competitiveness. Leaders will make some decisions that better position their institutions in the market (such as increasing selectivity or reducing class size) or capitalize on new sources of funds (such as creating an executive MBA program). Under the best of circumstances, these activities may not advance institutional diversity agendas, and in the worse cases, they may actually run counter to them. Market pressure is strong and resources are scarce, which means that costly programs driven by social needs may lose out. Building new programs or making changes that support the academic success of diverse students requires resources that may not be available. Institutional leaders will have to react in ways that strive to satisfy competing priorities and make changes that result in positive outcomes for both.

Summary

This short introduction has not explored all of the challenges facing American higher education that are demanding responses. Many others deserve reference, if only to give them some attention. Examples include increased accountability and its siblings assessment and quality assurance, the need to better fulfill the public service role expected of higher education, challenges to diversify the faculty ranks and explore alternative faculty employment arrangements, and pressure to respond to evolving economic competitiveness and workforce development needs. The fundamental premise of this argument suggests that the ability to take charge of change and intentionally set an institution's course is essentially the work of college and university leaders for the foreseeable future.

TOWARD TRANSFORMATION

Some, but not all, institutions will set their course for significant institution-wide change to attend to these evolving contexts. The challenge lies in their ability to pursue a major change agenda, one that is increasingly deep and pervasive and that will change their institutional cultures. For many institutions, making the necessary changes will go beyond an isolated approach to address a seemingly knowable problem. Instead, the solutions called for most likely will include integrated and intentional action by the institution as a whole and will require institutions to rethink key assumptions and beliefs and to develop new ways of operating.

For those institutions facing a complicated situation with multiple problems, the solution will be nothing short of institutional transformation. Although no particular, well-defined circumstance demands transformation, institutions facing a set of challenges that a single solution cannot address, that raise questions about whom the institution serves and what its effects should be, and that prompt the institution to examine multiple processes may suggest transformation.

The definition of transformation we use here was the cornerstone of the ACE project on which the present work is based (Eckel, Hill, & Green, 1998):

Transformation (1) alters the culture of the institution by changing underlying assumptions and overt institutional behaviors, processes, and structures; (2) is deep and pervasive, affecting the whole institution; (3) is intentional; and (4) occurs over time.

We learned that transformation requires processes different from other types of change, such as adding a new major, revising general education requirements, or implementing a new student information system. Although each of these changes has the potential to lead to profound alterations within a given unit, their circumscribed nature differentiates them from transformational change.

Transformation does not imply a complete overhaul of everything an institution does or stands for. It will not turn colleges or universities into elementary schools or bakeries. The historic social roles and the expectations of students, employers, policy makers, and faculty suggest that institutions, even those that undertake the greatest of transformations, will not find themselves unrecognizable. Colleges and universities that undertake transformation will alter the way in which they think about and conduct their basic functions of teaching and learning, scholarship and discovery, and engagement and service. However, they will remain true to their historic values and social roles.

Such a definition of transformation distinguishes itself both qualitatively and quantitatively from other kinds of change. We learned early in the project the importance of using clear and differentiated language when discussing various degrees of change. We also came to understand that the processes used to bring about major, deep, and widespread change differ from those strategies that affect other types of change. After observing, working with, and studying the twenty-three institutions that participated in the six-year ACE Project on Leadership and Institutional Transformation, we have identified a set of interrelated strategies common among those making the most progress toward transformation.

Transforming institutions relied on five primary or core strategies—senior administrative support, collaborative leadership, flexible vision, staff development, and visible action. These core strategies were linked to a host of supporting strategies. This second set of strategies, although not as essential to transformation as the first, contributed in important ways by helping to implement the core strategies. For example, important to the core strategy of senior administrative support were the supporting strategies of developing supportive structures throughout the institution, providing financial resources, creating incentives, developing an environment for shared leadership, and using external forces wisely to advance change.

A key part of transformation that we uncovered is the importance of helping people to think differently; creating new understandings and meanings is essential to deep and pervasive change. Finally, we learned that institutional culture shapes the process of transformation and that to effect transformation, leaders should become cultural analysts to understand the pitfalls and opportunities offered by their own culture. The subsequent chapters detail these findings and provide illustrations from project institutions.

THE ACE PROJECT ON LEADERSHIP AND INSTITUTIONAL TRANSFORMATION

The notion of transformation and the ideas in this book originated in the real-life challenges and successes (and struggles) of colleges and universities. This book is based on the experiences of twenty-three diverse colleges and universities that participated in the ACE Project on Leadership and Institutional Transformation.

The purpose of the five-and-a-half year project was threefold: (1) to help a group of diverse willing institutions set and make progress on their own agendas for large-scale change, (2) to assist these institutions to develop a reflective capacity to understand better their change processes and develop the capacity to change and change again when needed, and (3) to learn from the project institutions so that others outside of the project might benefit from their experiences, wisdom, successes, and failures. This book is part of the dissemination efforts.

The project, funded by the W. K. Kellogg Foundation originally for three-and-a-half years and then extended for two more years, was designed around the belief that institutions, through various processes involving faculty and administrative (and frequently student) leaders, had the capacity to advance internally set agendas for transformational change. ACE did not identify a set of issues that institutions should address or advocate particular agendas. Institutions were encouraged to take stock of their own circumstances and changing environments. We assisted in starting the project with each institution's own clear agenda for change, one that fit their individual context and was consistent with institutional purposes, histories, goals, and expectations. In some instances, administrators identified the problems and set the direction. At other institutions, faculty leadership primarily determined the change agenda. Other institutions drew on a combination of stakeholders. No clear pattern emerged about which processes were better. Successes and failures came from each of the three groups.

We strongly believed that the reason most institution-wide change failed was not for a lack of good ideas (as institutions are the intellectual homes of many smart and savvy people) but because of breakdowns in the process. Good ideas and best intentions get derailed because leaders do not pay enough attention to institutional norms, perceptions that differ across units, and people's feelings of worth and value. They rely on processes that are not inclusive in the right ways, are not transparent when they need to be, or tap the wrong people to fulfill important leadership roles. The project adopted a shorthand to differentiate its emphasis on the change process as "the how of change" from the "what of change," or content of the change agenda. This distinction reflected our belief that many good plans and intentions generated through significant work by many people frequently have little impact because leaders spend the majority of their time, energy, and focus on what they want to change, and the implementation process is an afterthought.

Project Structure

ACE solicited applications to participate in this project. It mailed an invitation to apply to approximately 450 of its 1,600 member institutions. Through a selection committee composed of institution presidents and association leaders, ACE selected 26 institutions from a pool of 110 applications (three of those institutions later opted out of the project's final two years, leaving the final 23 institutions). ACE sought to include institutions that reflected the diversity of American two- and four-year colleges and universities. It also attempted to select institutions that had a range of histories implementing change and innovation. Some were well-known innovators. Other institutions did not have that same track record of success and were just embarking on ambitious change. Still other institutions recognized that systemic problems existed, and that the external challenges were great, but did not know where to begin their work.

The twenty-six institutions selected included four community colleges, five liberal arts colleges, six comprehensive universities, six doctoral universities, and five research universities. Within that mix were three

Hispanic-serving institutions, a historically black college, and two women's colleges. The institutions represented geographic diversity and were a mix of public and private institutions. Appendix A lists the twenty-six institutions that originally participated in the project.

Each of the twenty-six institutions was asked to put together a project team to interact with ACE staff and project consultants who would conduct campus visits and facilitate project meetings. Institutions were encouraged to construct project teams in ways that worked best for their campuses and change agendas. However, we specified that the chief academic officer be a team member (although not necessarily the chair) and that at least half of the members be full-time faculty members. The individuals staffing the project were ACE staff from the Center for Institutional and International Initiatives, the Office of Minorities in Higher Education, and the Office of Women in Higher Education. Seasoned higher education administrators and experts worked as project consultants. The project staff visited each institution twice a year during the first three years and annually the last two years. They provided useful "outside eyes" and were asked to help institutions better understand their own institutional change processes, both successes and missteps. Campus site visits typically consisted of two days of focus groups and interviews with key campus change leaders to discuss the change process, their progress and struggles, and the insights institutions were gaining from their efforts.

In addition, we grouped the twenty-six institutions into smaller "clusters" of three to five similar institutions. The clusters met at project meetings twice a year for the first three years of the project and once a year during the last two years to share with one another their successes and challenges associated with the change process. The conversations at project meetings were facilitated by project staff and structured to encourage the sharing of insights. Some conversations were also organized to encourage sharing across the clusters of institutions. For example, frequently, members of institutional teams working on similar change topics, such as technology or faculty roles and rewards, conversed.

Additional information on the research methodology of this project appears in appendix B; however, each meeting and campus visit provided opportunities for ACE staff and project consultants to collect the information that underlies this book. In addition to site visit notes and project meeting summaries, all participating institutions completed written reports prior to each project meeting. Thus we collected six reports from institutions during the first three years of the project and two reports during the final two years.

Participating Project Institutions

For the twenty-six institutions participating in this project, the degrees of success varied. We identified how much progress toward transformation institutions made by visiting them at the beginning of the project and at the end and by interacting with them consistently throughout the project to capture the effects of their efforts over time. We categorized project institutions into three groups: transforming institutions, a middle group, and those that made adjustments.

Six of the participating institutions were clearly on the journey toward transformation. Compared with where they were when they began their concerted change efforts, these institutions could be considered "transformed," so deep and broad were the changes that had occurred. However, to those participating faculty and administrators, change was still very much a work in progress, and they readily acknowledged that success simply led to new challenges—and even more changes. Because most of these institutions had worked on their change agendas for more than six years (starting before the project began), their challenges were now second- and third-generation issues stimulated by earlier successes. Although transforming institutions often experienced setbacks along the way, such as challenges by faculty, funding downturns, and leadership transitions, they continued to work on the change agenda, however uneven their progress seemed at times. By identifying those institutions that made the most progress toward implementing their change agendas, we were able to classify some as *transforming institutions*. We termed them as *transforming* to indicate their own beliefs that the transformations they intended to effect were still very much under way. These institutions continued to face their share of people indifferent to change and some working actively against it. Nonetheless, the changes became deeply embedded over time, despite the efforts of those who wanted to derail change. We learned that five-and-a-half years is an inadequate period of time for most institutions to transform themselves.

About one-quarter of the participating institutions were what we term *adjusting*, having made a variety of improvements but no major changes. These institutions accomplished some change; however, they made the least amount of progress on their transformation agendas. More significant, their progress did not lead to changes in institutional culture. For some institutions, succeeding at adjustments met their goals. Once in the project, they rethought transformation, scaling back their intentions as they realized that major change would not benefit them as much as originally thought.

The final group of institutions, the remaining half, made some change that added up to more than adjustments. However, their processes tended to be either pervasive or deep, but not both. Time was clearly a factor for some institutions; although campus leaders may have established important foundations for meaningful change, the faculty may have needed more involvement in succeeding years to produce additional results. Continued progress toward transformation for most of these institutions in the middle ground is not guaranteed. Progress to date could be undone by any number of factors, such as a powerful coordinated resistance before the institution firmly established the change, a poorly handled leadership transition, or a diversion of attention and resources. Because our intent here is to understand the process of transformation, we focus most of this book on the six transforming institutions.[2]

Archdiocese University

Archdiocese University is a comprehensive, private Catholic-affiliated university of approximately ten thousand students located just outside a major urban area. It is the oldest Catholic postsecondary institution in the area. The university has long been prized for its commitment to undergraduate education founded on strong Christian values. More than two-thirds of its students come from the surrounding metropolitan area, and many of these students are first-generation. The university has approximately 350 full-time faculty who teach in six colleges and awards degrees in over forty-five disciplines at the bachelor's, master's, and doctoral levels.

Within its Catholic context, Archdiocese is working at transforming its undergraduate experience with a particular emphasis on technology. Faculty and administrative leaders recognized that many of their students enter the institution with highly developed skills of listening and repeating, which in their opinion do little to advance "learning." They viewed their challenge as "making students independent, critical, and technologically sophisticated learners." A hallmark of its efforts is its mobile computing program, which provides all undergraduates with a laptop computer, and the creation of a corresponding institution-wide infrastructure to support transportable technology. The mobile computing program is designed to integrate technology into the classroom and allow students ubiquitous access to powerful learning tools. As its leaders stress, that project is designed to go beyond simply putting a laptop into the hands of its students.

Civic State University

Civic State University is a research-intensive university located in a metropolitan area. Its five colleges and schools offer over one hundred bachelor's, master's, and doctoral degrees to the approximately fourteen thousand students enrolled. Close to eight hundred faculty teach these students. The majority of students are undergraduates, of which only 40 percent are younger than twenty-five years old. Less than half of all students attend full-time. The majority of students live off campus (89 percent), and approximately 40 percent transferred to the institution. The campus offered its first degrees in the mid-1950s.

Civic State is working to adopt an urban-centered mission and to implement a "coherent and cohesive program of integrated learning experiences" through its general education curriculum. A primary focus of its efforts was on rethinking faculty roles to best serve the urban university agenda. The institution is recrafting its identity to become an urban campus. As one person put it, the idea of an urban institution "goes beyond location" and concerns itself with the notions reflected in the new institutional motto: "Let Knowledge Serve the City."

Metropolitan University

Metropolitan University, a private, urban research university, is revising its curriculum to achieve the learning objectives common to general education through the major. The initiative's goal is to provide students with a more coherent education. Through this initiative, known as the Common Academic Charter (CAC), faculty across the colleges are crafting general education outcomes that are connected to all curricular components, such as liberal arts courses, disciplinary courses, and noncourse experiences modules.

The pressure for change came internally from faculty who recognized that the current structure of general education was simply not working and externally from an accreditation review that cited the institution for its lack of common educational experiences. Campus administrators were not surprised at the curriculum's fragmentation because it reflected the high degree of independence of Metropolitan's colleges and departments. An earlier attempt to create a university-wide core curriculum failed in part because, according to some, the professional programs resisted adding new required courses to already highly structured curricula.

At the same time as receiving the critical accreditation report highlighting the curricular problem, the institution faced a 30 percent drop in enrollment that, in turn, created financial hard times for the tuition-driven institution. In addition, the institution recently was reclassified from a Doctoral II to a Research II institution in the former Carnegie classification system, jumping two categories. In response to the report and reclassification, one person noted, "While research and teaching is not an either/or proposition, the desire for upward mobility in the research world often finds institutions sending conflicting messages about its core values." These were the challenges facing a new president and provost.

Middle State University

Middle State University is a public doctoral university located in a small town. It enrolls approximately eighteen thousand students, of whom slightly more than half are women. Close to 90 percent of its students come from in state, and 1 percent are international. Approximately 40 percent live on campus. The university has seven academic colleges and a graduate school with more than 870 full-time faculty. Included among the colleges are architecture, business, fine arts, communications, and applied sciences and technology. In the course of its hundred-year history, it was transformed from a teacher's college to a doctoral university.

Middle State is endeavoring to integrate technology into the core of its teaching and learning process. This initiative had the ambitious goal of having the entire faculty involved in rethinking their courses and curricula around infusing technology to enrich the undergraduate student experience. The intent was to "develop a technology consciousness" that would transcend all courses, instruction, and learning and become woven into the fabric of the institution.

Midwest College

Midwest College is located in a small, rural community. The majority of its nine hundred students are traditional-age undergraduates. They come to the institution mostly from small suburban and rural high schools; however, Midwest recently began recruiting students from the large urban schools. Many of its students are first generation. The majority of students live on campus. Greek-lettered organizations and athletics play important roles in the social lives of students. In the late 1980s and early 1990s, the campus faced high faculty attrition: over 20 percent per year of its approximately seventy-two full-time faculty either retired or moved to other institutions. Enrollments stagnated, and a racial incident sent the campus into crisis, leading to the president's resignation and a change in the leadership of the board of trustees. A new president was hired to return the college to solid footing.

The focus of Midwest College's change agenda was to align its educational practices with its newly articulated values and the goals, "Education for Individual and Social Responsibility." It was the intent of campus leaders to create a new institutional culture and curriculum around "preparing graduates of character and competence: individuals not only prepared to enter their chosen field, but also who understood what it means to be a responsible person in today's society and who were capable of acting on that understanding."

Sunshine Community College

Sunshine Community College is a four-campus community college of approximately fifty-four thousand students, located within a growing metropolitan area. It serves two of the fastest-growing counties in the state. The average age of its credit-seeking students is twenty-five. Close to 70 percent of its students enroll in credit courses, and more than half of its students are enrolled in at least one developmental (remedial) course. It has 326 full-time faculty and approximately 1,100 part-time instructors. It generates significant outside federal and state grants to support its educational programs, with a large portion of aid received under Title III.

Sunshine is attempting to move from being a faculty- or teaching-centered institution to being a learning-centered institution. The college noted in a report to ACE: "The decision to focus on learning represented a shift in college focus from the activity of teaching to the result of that activity—learning. The college had for several years focused on supporting teaching. If teachers were supported, it was assumed that learning was supported and was occurring. However, renewed internal and external attention focused attention on the results of the teaching process."

CONCLUSION

Transformational change is a complex and difficult undertaking, something we learned by working with the twenty-three institutions seeking to implement such change over six years. We present this book as a way to help other campus leaders, be they faculty, administrators, trustees, or students, understand better the transformation in higher education and to give them the insight to make wise decisions.

In the next chapter, we describe transformation in depth, compare it to other types of change, and describe a template that can help leaders chart transformation on their own campuses.

NOTES

1. These scenarios are based on actual institutions; however, certain elements have been changed to attempt anonymity.

2. We identify each of the transforming institutions through a pseudonym.

CHAPTER

Defining and
Charting Transformation

Language is important both for understanding and for implementing major change. This chapter clarifies some of the language of change and transformation and is intended as a guide to help chart the various waters of change in higher education. It describes transformational change in depth, compares it to other types of change occurring in academe, and provides a template for understanding the extent to which institutions are on their way to transformation.

TRANSFORMATIONAL CHANGE

In chapter 1, we defined transformational change as affecting institutional cultures, as deep and pervasive, as intentional, and as occurring over time. We offer a tight definition of transformation to stress that it is a particular type of change that has associated with its implementation a unique cluster of strategies and activities. Understanding the attributes of transformational change and its associated activities helps institutional leaders determine the extent to which transformation is necessary and the strategies to bring it about.[1]

First, transformation is about *changing institutional cultures*. It requires a major shift in the many cultural elements of an institution. Culture is the dominant patterns of shared assumptions, values, beliefs, ideologies, and meanings that people have about their organization that shapes what individuals do and how they think (Peterson & Spencer, 1991). It is the invisible glue that creates a common framework that holds together an institution—the institution-wide patterns of perceiving, thinking, and feeling and the collective assumptions and common interpretive frameworks (Kuh & Whitt, 1988; Schein, 1992; Tierney, 1991). Because institutional culture determines what is important, how certain tasks should be and are accomplished, who leads and how, and what legitimate decisions are made and by whom, it plays an important role in shaping the process of transformation and is recast as an outcome. The cultures of many colleges and universities are composites of various subcultures that are defined by their own values, activities, norms, and beliefs. However, even institutions dominated by strong subcultures share, to some extent, common elements that appear across subcultures and that help to define the institution as an organization. In addition, institutions, although unique in their own right, share cultural elements with other institutions (Bergquist, 1992).

An institution cannot make major change without altering at least some parts of its culture. However, transformational change in higher education is unlikely to lead to a completely new culture, as many elements of various academic subcultures transcend institutional boundaries and are shaped by strong disciplinary alliances as well as by other external forces, such as accreditation and professional and disciplinary societies (Alpert, 1991). Institutions share common professionally developed beliefs and norms to which their employees are extensively socialized during graduate school and that influence behaviors inside institutions (Mintzberg, 1983). Thus, some elements of an institution's culture will change, others will be reshaped, and still others will remain steadfast. Part of the transformation process is determining what elements of an institution's culture work well, which components should and will remain consistent, and what parts are no longer working well or are preventing more beneficial elements from taking hold.

One can think about institutional culture as composed of three layers: the top layer is the most visible artifacts of an organization; the middle layer is the espoused values; and the innermost core is the underlying assumptions (Schein, 1992). The artifacts are the concrete elements of a culture. They are the products, activities, processes, rules, and structures that reflect an institution's culture. Artifacts include, among other things, insider language, myths and stories, mission statements and strategic plans, rituals and ceremonies (such as freshmen convocation), reward structures and their implementation, and organizational hierarchies. For example, at one project institution, some key artifacts associated with its transformation agenda to improve student learning included (1) the orientation schedule, which articulated what new students should learn about entering the college, (2) the student handbook and a widely available list of learning resources, (3) faculty development activities that did not include workshops on new pedagogies, (4) hiring and promotion policies that paid scant attention to teaching effectiveness, and (5) newly reorganized student resource centers, which included academic advising, career development, tutoring services, and adult student reentry programs.

The second layer of culture contains the espoused values, which are the articulated beliefs about what is "good," what "works," and what is "right." Examples include statements such as the following: "We develop citizen-leaders," "We value public engagement and service to our communities," "We promote useful knowledge." Mission statements and strategic plans are rife with such declarations. They send important messages about what the institution publicly stands for and what it actively promotes. For instance, in the previous example, the new student orientation and its agenda send important messages about the perceived needs of new students. At orientation, students hear and experience institutional values in action. Other values are communicated by the structure of offices and activities at the college. Housing the reentry program for adult students in the student resource center sends the message that these students are part of the mainstream, not a marginalized subgroup. Prominently displaying tutoring services and making them readily available conveys institutional beliefs about retention and student success.

The underlying assumptions make up the innermost core of institutional culture. These are the taken-for-granted beliefs that are rarely examined or questioned because they are so deeply ingrained that people are usually not readily aware of them. These underlying beliefs guide actions and shape priorities and practices. Underlying assumptions are most readily identified when they are in conflict with espoused beliefs (Argyris, 1994; Schein, 1992). For example, an institution can state publicly through memos, policies, view books, and other materials that ensuring the success of its diverse students is important, yet it can have practices (often unwritten and frequently unnoticed) that result in lower graduation rates for students of color. Transformational change involves surfacing and changing those underlying assumptions—as well as changing corresponding espoused values and artifacts—that are incongruent with the intended new direction of the institution.

Second, transformational change *affects the whole institution* and is *deep and pervasive*. Transformation is not about addressing discrete problems or implementing new programs. Its depth captures how profoundly a change affects behaviors, ways of thinking, structures, policies, beliefs, and practices. Transformation, as we have defined it, touches the underlying assumptions as well as the accompanying values and artifacts. The deeper the change, the more it is woven into the fabric of the institution and the greater its penetration and effect. Pervasiveness, on the other hand, refers to the extent to which the change permeates the institution. The more pervasive the change, the more far-reaching its touch, affecting different parts of the institution including academic and nonacademic units, service units, and the infrastructure.

Third, transformation is *intentional*. It is undertaken to generate purposeful and desirable outcomes (although it also generates unintended consequences). Our definition does not account for changes that are serendipitous or unintended. Transformation, as we use the concept here, does not simply "happen." We acknowledge that institutions are continually buffeted by changing environments that can sometimes lead to profound changes, but that is not transformation. Transformation includes conscious decisions by the institution. The first decision is to act, and the second purposeful choice is the direction of those actions. Transformation requires leaders (both formal and informal) to make a conscious set of decisions. However, often these intentional decisions are strongly shaped by external realities, such as changes in the environment, or in response to new mandates and budgetary pressures or to new opportunities.

That said, intentionality does not mean that leaders must, as a first step, have as a goal change that is transformational in its depth and magnitude. We observed over the course of the project that a variety of changes can lead to transformation, as they cascade and build on one another. Institutions can back into transformation as easily as leaders can set out for it. Nonetheless, no matter which path institutions follow, institutional leaders must still have a purpose to guide their efforts.

Finally, transformation occurs *over time*. We differentiate transformation from revolutionary change, which happens quickly. Major change takes time. Creating a new institutional culture, implementing changes that have a deep and pervasive impact, and generating sought-after results will not occur quickly in most instances. Frequently, transformational change will happen only as the cumulative effect of a multitude of changes in the curriculum and cocurriculum, and across numerous departments and units, some of which are more strongly linked than other changes. Colleges and universities are not structured, governed, or led in ways that, for the most part, allow for rapid change. Their complexity, diffused decision making, and multiple purposes make change difficult and multifaceted and, thus, time consuming. Higher education is unlikely to witness any "big bangs." The speed of change has little to do with its magnitude or impact, although critics like to focus on the slow pace of academic change.

TRANSFORMATION AS OPPOSED TO OTHER TYPES OF CHANGE

Transformational change becomes even clearer when contrasted with other types of change. First, this section compares transformational change to other types of less deep and pervasive change. Then it contrasts transformation with innovation implementation, adaptation, and strategic change, other types of change common to higher education.

Within the ACE project, we differentiated transformation from three other types of change—adjustment, isolated change, and far-reaching change—by contrasting these changes by their depth and pervasiveness. Using these two characteristics of transformation as the axis of a simple matrix helped us differentiate transformational change from adjustments, isolated change, and far-reaching change. The matrix shown in figure 2.1 depicts the changes and their relationship to one another along these two dimensions.

The first quadrant, adjustment, refers to modifications or extensions that improve existing practices. These are the revisions, renewals, and redesigns of current activities, processes, and practices or the introduction of new elements that have a limited effect. Adjustments do not lead to drastic or deep changes, nor do they extend very far across an institution. Within colleges and universities, adjustments are made continually. For

Figure 2.1
Typology of Change

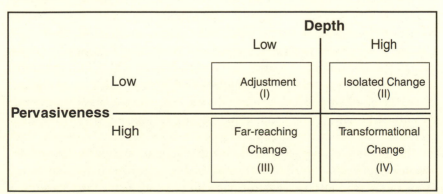

		Depth	
		Low	High
Pervasiveness	Low	Adjustment (I)	Isolated Change (II)
	High	Far-reaching Change (III)	Transformational Change (IV)

instance, faculty introduce new texts and try new pedagogies in various courses, colleges implement new advising procedures for their majors, and residence halls or science laboratories adopt new safety practices. The faculty and administrators at one liberal arts college in the project made a series of important adjustments to its curriculum and pedagogies. They developed a well-received first-year course, which was interdisciplinary, that focused on different ways of knowing. The course generated unheard-of enthusiasm among faculty for the general education curriculum and put the ideas of interdisciplinary knowledge in practice. However, the new course directly affected only the few faculty teaching sections of the course (although it did involve all first-year students); it did not alter other elements of the general education curriculum or the majors; and it resulted in little structural or behavioral changes across the institution. The course was an important change for the campus, but its effects were limited.

The second quadrant, isolated change, is deep but limited to one unit or program or to a particular area. Because it is deep, isolated change implies a shift in values and assumptions that underlie the "normal" way of operating. It results in people not only thinking differently but also acting differently. However, isolated change has little or no impact on other units or areas. An example of isolated change is an academic department that adopts internationalization as central to its mission. The new mission leads to changes in promotion and tenure criteria as well as in hiring priorities that place a premium on international activities, scholarship, and teaching. Students study and conduct senior theses on international topics. Courses use the Internet and other telecommunications tools to incorporate international dimensions and perspectives. Faculty revise syllabi to include readings and scholarship from foreign scholars. The department encourages study abroad for all students and creates various options to fit busy student schedules. It supports faculty exchange during the summer and brings in foreign scholars for semester residencies. The department creates an award for faculty innovation around internationalizing currently offered courses, and it raises new money to support faculty research abroad. These changes add up to a department fundamentally different than previously; new values, priorities, and practices suggest deep change. Nevertheless, the changes have not spread to other departments within the college, remaining unique to their immediate location.

Far-reaching change, the third quadrant, is pervasive but not deep. Pervasiveness refers to the extent to which a change is extensive within the institution. The more extensive the change, the further it crosses unit boundaries and affects a range of units and programs. However, far-reaching change is not very deep. It has little effect on values, beliefs, and practices. For example, a change may require the syllabi of all courses to be placed on the Internet. The new policy touches every course and the faculty who teach them; however, it does not change their pedagogies or alter their course assignments. It does little to alter beliefs or practices regarding technology in the classroom.

The fourth quadrant is transformational change, change that is both deep and pervasive. Transformational change is isolated change that is far-reaching. It is the internationalization example discussed for the second quadrant, but across the whole institution, touching most, if not all, units, departments, and programs. Transformation is not about fixing discrete problems or adjusting current activities. The depth of the change affects those underlying assumptions that tell an institution what is important; what to do, why, and how; and what to produce. Its pervasiveness suggests that transformation is a collective, institution-wide phenomenon, although it may occur one unit (or one person) at a time. We discuss in more detail later in this chapter institutional examples of transformation.

The rest of this section explores the ways in which transformation compares to other types of change prevalent in higher education—innovation implementation, adaptation, and strategic change. Depending on definitions and conceptual frameworks, these three types of change, together with transformation, may have tremendous conceptual overlap and are not always sharply distinguished from one another in the literature. That said, we define them succinctly here to enable comparison and further clarify the concept of transformation.

Innovation Implementation

An innovation is a new specific tangible product, process, service, or procedure that is intentionally introduced and expected to have positive, if not significant, benefits for the institution (Leifer, O'Connor, & Rice, 2001). It pushes the organization to respond beyond its currently established routines (Mone, McKinley, & Barker, 1998). An innovation is adopted after leaders recognize the potential contributions of the new activity to the organization. Adoption occurs prior to innovation implementation, which happens when employees become committed to the innovation and use it appropriately (Klein & Sorra, 1996). First, decision makers determine that the innovation is appropriate for the institution. Second, the actual implementation of that new product, service, or procedure occurs. For example, when institutional leaders determine that a particular posttenure review process is needed, it becomes adopted, which reflects the fit of the innovation to the institution's needs. The subsequent use of the posttenure process by various academic departments is the implementation of the innovation. Innovation implementation is ultimately about changing certain behaviors of a critical group of individuals, if not the organization as a whole (Klein & Sorra, 1996). The implementation of an innovation is shaped by institutional culture, as norms, values, and goals influence the degree to which various innovations are more or less desirable and implemented (Levine, 1980).

Prior to innovation implementation is its adoption. Rogers (1962) offered the classic innovation diffusion and adoption theory in the early 1960s. His model is composed of five stages: awareness, interest, evaluation, trial, and adoption. He posits that the first stage is *awareness*, in which the individual is exposed to the innovation but neither has adequate information to determine its value nor is motivated enough to seek additional evidence. The second phase is *interest*: individuals become more attracted to the innovation and seek additional information. The third stage is *evaluation*: individuals consider applying the innovation to their present and future circumstances. During the fourth stage, the *trial state*, the innovation is implemented on a small scale, making a "dry run." At the fifth stage, *adoption*, the innovation is adopted fully.

In reality, the actual implementation of the innovation may not be so straightforward. Instead, researchers suggest, these processes are marked by sporadic stops and starts, are unpredictable, and do not adhere to linear paths (Leifer, O'Connor, & Rice, 2001). Innovations spread not only by intentional decisions within the organization but through mimicry and imitation, and because of serendipity and desperation (O'Neill, Pouder, & Buchholtz, 1998). Klein and Sorra (1996) suggest that two key factors in the efficacy of implementation are the organizational climate—the employees' perceptions of events, procedures, behaviors, and practices that are rewarded and expected—and the extent to which individuals within the organization view the innovation as consistent with their values, a belief that goes beyond seeing the innovation as more than simply a means to avoid punishment.

Adaptation

Adaptation refers to deliberate modifications or adjustments on the part of the organization or its units in response to changes in the external environment (Cameron, 1991). The changes are motivated from without, rather than from within—for example, with administrative goals. Adaptations are adjustments that respond to a lack of fit with the changing external world, in which the organization restores equilibrium between environmental demands and internal structures (Gumport & Sporn, 1999). However, adaptation is not always simply in reaction to changes in environments; it can be proactive or anticipatory (Cameron, 1991). Adaptation can be either intentional or emergent and nonplanned (Maassen, Neave, & Jongbloed, 1999). Adaptation can include changes in structures—which can be broadly defined to include degree programs—and changes in the size, shape, and composition of various groups of administrators, students, or faculty to reflect, for example, newly developed programs or to respond to new laws affecting the institution (Maassen, Neave, & Jongbloed, 1999). Gumport and Sporn (1999) discuss the expanded role of administration as a result of university adaptation to increasingly complex environments.

Adaptation typically refers to a process rather than a single event (Cameron, 1991). The process occurs over time, is shaped by various environmental influences, and is evolutionary (Morgan, 1986). Adaptation reflects the ideas—such as systems, openness, and homeostasis (Sporn, 1999)—of population ecology, evolutionary and biological models of change, institutional isomorphism, and resource dependence (Kezar, 2001; Gumport & Sporn, 1999). The systemic nature of adaptation refers to the interdependent relationship of the organization with its environment and its linkages among units, so that changes felt in one area have an effect elsewhere within the organization, sometimes strongly, other times weakly. Openness characterizes the relationship between the environment and the internal activities of the organization and describes the organization's strong dependence on its environment. The notion of homeostasis is the self-regulatory balancing process through which organizations seek equilibrium between the system and its environment (Sporn, 1999).

Adaptation may occur at either the organizational or a subunit level. The loosely coupled nature of colleges and universities—in which units are only weakly connected, information travels slowly and indirectly, and coordination is minimal—allows for added adaptability. Weick (1983) suggests that these characteristics give colleges and universities an advantage over tightly coupled institutions in their ability to respond to changed environments in the following four ways. First, he notes that in loosely coupled organizations, the organization as a whole does not have to respond to the environment. Instead, individual units can react. These individual units are more sensitive to detailed and nuanced changes in the environment than is the institution as a whole. For example, a college of education is aware of statewide deliberations about teacher preparation, leaving other units in the institution to attend to different local needs. Second, the loosely coupled nature of institutions allows for greater sensitivity to external forces, important to adaptation. Not all aspects of an institution need to focus on the same elements in the external environment. Third, the loose coupling also allows individual units to adapt to changes without creating disequilibrium for the whole institution. Thus, the college of education can adapt to a new teacher certification examination without prompting the physics department to overhaul its undergraduate curriculum. Finally, if the adaptation undertaken in one part of the loosely coupled organization is a poor choice, the weak linkages among units seal off the dysfunction so it does not infiltrate other areas of the organization.

However, the loosely coupled nature of colleges and universities creates challenges to adaptation as well. Their independence means that they attend to different components of the environments. Thus, what may be an impending crisis for one unit may be barely perceptible elsewhere in the same institution. Second, although agile independently, units lack coordination and cannot respond collectively and consistently to changes in the environment. Finally, various units react at different speeds, as information travels inconsistently and indirectly.

Strategic Change

As new for-profit institutions, corporate universities, and foreign universities enter the traditional U.S. higher education arena (Adleman, 2000; Newman & Couturier, 2001), making oneself distinct from these new competitors may require an institution to undertake specific changes that alter its positioning in the competitive environment. This process, called strategic change, occurs through altering the areas or fields and markets in which the organization operates (Boeker, 1997; Rajagopalan & Spreitzer, 1996). It changes the focus of an organization's strategy. Strategic change is about acting on a "vision of the direction that the business [or institution] should pursue" (Mintzberg, 1994, p. 107). It affects the institution's realized patterns of activity and will change the programs and services it offers, at least to some extent, the students it recruits, the degrees it awards, and the research it conducts and where it disseminates or applies that research. However, rarely will strategic change abandon completely one set of strategies for another because colleges and universities fulfill important social roles where continuity is important (Salipante & Golden-Biddle, 1995).

Examples of strategic change include the introduction of a set of new degree programs, such as in high-tech or multimedia fields, and, in an opposite situation, the closure of certain academic programs. An institution may also undertake strategic change if it alters its mission from serving predominately traditional-age students to focusing on adult learning, or from one that has been predominately campus based to one that adopts a Web-based delivery strategy and targets new student markets correspondingly.

Strategic change is not about strategic planning, a topic familiar to most institutional leaders; nor is it about alignment of activities with objectives or even plans and planning, such as is the focus of most strategic planning activities (Mintzberg, 1994). Neither does strategic change require strategic planning. Presley and Leslie (1999) noted in a study of strategic change at institutions facing imminent financial crisis that although institutions changed strategies, "none engaged in what one might recognize as a standardized textbook formal strategic planning exercise" (p. 229).

In colleges and universities, and other organizations that operate like them, institutional strategy is a composite of decisions and choices made not only at the board and administrative level but also at the collegial level (i.e., in committees, departments, and the campus senate) and at the individual professional level, for instance, where academics identify the means and focus of each course and determine their own research agendas (Hardy, Langley, Mintzberg, & Rose, 1983). The ambiguous and often unclear goals of higher education (what exactly is academic excellence, citizenship development, or service to the state?) and the autonomy of its professionals mean that a tightly cast strategy formulated at the top is unlikely to win faculty support. Instead, institutional strategy reflects the actual patterns of decisions and activities that occur over time. A new strategy is as likely to emerge from a set of loosely coordinated decisions and activities as it is to be deliberate (Mintzberg, 1987). An institution may find itself with an emergent strategy on urban issues, for example, started within one academic year because its college of education received a multimillion dollar grant to improve urban education; its architecture department hires three new faculty who specialize in historic preservation, urban renewal, and housing for the poor; and its public affairs program launches a high-profile lecture series on cities and civic leadership. The strategy of any single college or university is determined more by the steam of ongoing activities than by anything else.

Strategic change, thus, is about reshaping the patterns of decisions and activities. This frequently happens through a series of small "learning" steps intended to test the environment and the institution's place in it (Rajagopalan & Spreitzer, 1996). These small steps eventually make a cumulative impact through the work of individual professionals or groups of professionals who convince the institution to undertake particular initiatives, such as implementing a new degree program. Cumulative impacts also occur when central administrators work discretely to persuade people to do things differently (Mintzberg, 1983). Savvy and successful administrators can rarely impose their will on the professorate because they rely on faculty support to get things done (Birnbaum, 1992). As one former president put it, "If there is an issue at hand that the faculty cares deeply about and you can't persuade them, you certainly can't bulldoze them" (Walker, 1979, p. 10).

Differentiating Transformational Change

Transformational change, although it shares some elements with these other types of change, is itself unique. For instance, innovation implementation concerns itself predominantly with a specific tangible product, service, or procedure, but it does not have the same breadth or depth of transformation. That said, transformational change can, and in most cases does, include a variety of innovations. One could not consider transformational change associated with teaching and learning without acknowledging the importance of various pedagogical innovations. However, each innovation tends to have a limited effect and is used by a constrained set of individuals. For example, implementing computer-based models to demonstrate particular chemistry principles is an innovation most likely used by professors in chemistry and in related areas such as chemical engineering or biochemistry. However, innovation and transformation do share some characteristics. Both can be responses to internal desires or outside pressures, or a combination of both. An institution's culture, norms, and values shape both. Finally, to be successful, innovation and transformation must both be consistent with institutional needs.

Transformation is also distinct from adaptation in a number of ways. First, adaptation may very well be local; it does not have to be institutional, unlike the breadth of transformation. Second, it also may lack intentionality. Some theories of adaptation (population ecology, for example) suggest that responding to environmental changes may occur reactively, without sought-after objectives beyond institutional survival and environmental stasis. "Most organizations adapt, therefore, not because of intelligent or creative managerial action but by the random and evolutionary development of characteristics that are compatible with the environment" (Cameron, 1991, p. 286). However, other theories of adaptation suggest that managerial influence exists. Adaptation and transformational change share some characteristics as well. Both are ongoing processes and not single events. Both include responding to environmental changes. But transformation as we view it tends to couple outside pressure with internal desires. One set of pressures without the other may provide insufficient energy to sustain transformation.

Finally, transformation differs from strategic change. Strategic change, for example, does not suggest that an institution will change its culture or that the change will have a deep or widespread impact. Strategic change may simply be extending current activities to new areas or markets. For instance, it may include repackaging existing courses into a new consolidated degree program, or it could entail taking current degree offerings to a new market via technology. However, this example does not suggest that moving toward a Web-based degree program might not have other effects, intended or not, on the institution. Strategic change may not be comprehensive, but it has the potential to be. It also may not have the same degree of intentionality as transformational change because, in higher education, strategic change most often comes about through loosely coordinated activities. Transformation and strategic change do have commonalties. They both occur through small steps that add up to larger effects, and both require changes in decisions and activities that most likely occur over time. Finally, both types of change are responses to changing environments.

INDICATING TRANSFORMATION

In addition to defining transformation and contrasting it to other types of change, having a framework to determine the extent to which a change agenda is transformational helps put the concept of transformation into relief.[2] Understanding the process of transformation depends on differentiating the strategies that led to transformation from those that did not.

Using Schein's (1992) work on culture as a starting point, we developed a template that encompassed structural and cultural elements to determine the extent to which institutions were on their way to transformation. The experiences of project institutions helped us further refine the template. We recognized institutions to be well on their way to transformation when most, if not all, of the structural and cultural markers described below were easily recognizable.

To add up to transformation, the following structural and cultural markers had to be aligned, mutually reinforcing, and reflect progress in a common direction. One marker by itself, or even in conjunction with a few others, did not indicate transformation. Rather, transformation was evidenced by a set of interrelated, clustered markers. For example, an institution seeking to transform itself so that it ensures the academic success of all its diverse students may develop an important and successful freshman-year program. By itself, that program will only be a single indicator in a potential series of aligned intentional changes that reflects the institution-wide focus and commitment. A first-year program, even if comprehensive and accompanied by consistently espoused values, does not indicate transformation.

Structural Evidence

Structural evidence is a set of indicators composed of those familiar concrete markers that can be counted and measured and compared to baseline information. Transformation, we observed, is evidenced by the presence of most of these visible markers, and by a sense of synergy and connection among them. However, without the accompanying cultural markers described in the next section, they are insufficient to suggest transformation. We used the following structural markers:

- *Changes to the curriculum*. Whereas typical curricular change can be relatively minor (changing the number of science courses or adding a diversity or culture course), transformational change altered the types of knowledge presented through the curriculum, the ways in which the curriculum was organized, the central principles of what it intended to accomplish, and who was responsible for delivering particular curricular goals.
- *Changes in pedagogies*. Just as the curriculum changed, so did the pedagogies and delivery methods. The traditional array of lectures, discussion sessions, and seminars was supplemented by alternative teaching methods, such as collaborative work, Web-based learning, and learning communities.
- *Changes in student learning and assessment practices*. Institutions could articulate and demonstrate improvements in student learning and in learning outcomes assessment practices. They adopted multiple strategies, which frequently included portfolio assessment.
- *Changes in policies*. Institutions aligned their policies with their goals and articulated values. Among the key policies that were modified to support

transformation were merit pay and annual evaluations; hiring, promotion, and tenure; program review; faculty development and travel; and information technology. Some institutions developed policies that encouraged community engagement. They rewarded classroom experiences that had direct community ties and created merit-pay programs that encouraged scholarship that explicitly addressed local problems.

- *Changes in budgets*. Without corresponding shifts in the ways leaders allocate finances, good ideas may wither for lack of resources. Transformation required realigning budgets with new priorities and objectives. Sometimes, leaders found new sources of money; at other times, they reallocated existing resources.

- *New departments and institutional structures*. To do new things, institutions created new departments and institutional structures. Examples included centers for teaching excellence and units responsible for community service and outreach. The new units typically had their own budgets and staff, were responsible for certain functions, and frequently acted as clearinghouses of information and centers of coordination of campuswide efforts. Often, faculty leaders were tapped (and given release time) to lead these new units.

- *New decision-making structures*. Institutions no longer relied solely on well-worn traditions and patterns of decision making and problem solving. They learned that familiar methods led to expected (and habitual) solutions. To develop new solutions, institutions developed and tapped different decision-making structures that led to creative ideas and courses of action. For some institutions, it meant creating new ad hoc structures. For others, it meant incorporating ad hoc task forces into formal governance processes.

Attitudinal and Cultural Evidence

However much change was visible through the structural evidence, that evidence did not by itself suggest transformational change. Because transformation is about changing cultures, an additional set of evidence was needed to identify the cultural impact of transformation. These cultural markers signaled attitudinal and cultural shifts that suggested that an institution had accomplished more than surface change; it had developed new capacities and a new set of beliefs and assumptions regarding what it should be doing and how it should be going about it. These more subtle signs of transformation are not the markers commonly used by accrediting teams, legislatures, or boards of trustees. They are far more difficult to pinpoint and without the corresponding structural evidence can indicate superficial change. Campus leaders readily pointed out that new rhetoric

could exist without a corresponding deep change. Slogans that purport
new values and beliefs and statements about reorganized priorities can
mean little. It is quite another thing to permeate campus norms and
beliefs. We used the following cultural markers:

- *Changes in the ways groups or individuals interact with one another.* Institutions created new patterns of interactions; they found ways to connect
  people from different units who had not previously structured opportunities to work together, generating sources of new ideas and energy. For
  example, some institutions brought student affairs professionals to the
  table as educational peers rather than as a group responsible simply for
  "extracurricular" activities. Institutions created and fostered changed relationships between faculty-staff and students. Transforming institutions
  discovered and reinforced new ways for faculty and students to interact
  both inside and outside the classroom. These relationships were consistent with stated values and were reinforced by key policies, structures,
  and mind-sets. Examples include joint student-faculty research, student
  participation in campus decision making, and faculty-led service-learning
  experiences.

- *Changes in the language the campus used to talk about itself.* A different
  institutional self-image was a marker of cultural transformation. New
  language and self-concepts evolved over time until the shared terminology was widespread and became part of the institutional fabric. For
  example, some institutions that were one-time research university aspirants found pride in describing their new roles and niches with different terminology that expressed the new-found role they played in their
  cities and states. Their language reflected their pride in their service-based mission grounded in research and teaching, and it left behind their
  old research-university language.

- *Changes in the types of conversations.* The conversations on campus
  changed both in terms of who was at the table (different players from
  inside the institution and new partners from outside of it, particularly
  at urban institutions) and in the substance of the conversations. These
  new and different conversations reflected new priorities and new commitments. New topics found themselves on a majority of agendas, dominating campus conversations.

- *Old arguments abandoned.* A marker of new attitudes and beliefs was the
  willingness to abandon old arguments, such as "We can't do this because
  . . ." or "We tried this and it failed" as unsuitable. Old reasons for not
  acting often did not fit new realities because the contexts, challenges,
  and situations had changed. The willingness to take a fresh look signaled
  important shifts in institutional norms, beliefs, and culture. (Of course,
  this marker does not mean that new arguments did not surface: differences of opinion are part and parcel of academic life).

- *New relationships with stakeholders*. No institution can undergo profound change without the involvement of such stakeholders as trustees, alumni and donors, community groups, local businesses, and foundations. Transformation led to new types of relationships with these long-term stakeholders. Transformation also helped forge new relationships with nontraditional stakeholders, such as community agencies, local businesses, and civic groups.

These frameworks, although not providing "hard," indisputable data that institutions were transforming, provide adequate evidence of substantive change both in the concrete and cultural characteristics of institutions. It is not the intent of this book to prove that transformation occurred or did not occur, or to predict if and when an institution will be transformed. We can, however, safely say that some project institutions made substantially more progress than others did. We are confident that we know which institutions are further ahead of the change curve than others, giving us a set of institutions from which to draw our conclusions.

Determining Evidence of Transformation

Changes that occurred at two of the six transforming institutions are described in this section. Because the changes were sufficiently deep and pervasive, describing each of the six would take unwarranted space. We think the two descriptions, admittedly partial, provide representative evidence of transformation.

Archdiocese University

Archdiocese University, a private Catholic institution, launched its efforts to transform undergraduate education through the infusion of technology, particularly laptop computers, to restructure and enhance the learning experience. The use of mobile computing led to a range of significant changes that added up to a new campus culture. First, mobile computing led to new pedagogies in a wide range of majors and the core curriculum. All students are guaranteed at least two core curriculum courses that are technology intensive. The presence of laptops in the classrooms and residence halls challenged faculty to think differently about the ways in which they taught and created new opportunities for students to actively engage with course content.

The infrastructure needed to support this effort led to changes in budgeting. The administration used $5 million from its quasi-endowment to jumpstart its efforts. It also reconfigured tuition and financial aid to in-clude the costs of the computers for all students (and replace the computer after the student's second year). To support such an expensive endeavor, the institution not only found new money but also reallocated existing funds. Agreeing upon and then purchasing common software led to other effects. For example, the institution could not support four different kinds of software for statistics. When faculty came together from different de-partments to identify common software needs, they began discussions about teaching and shared questions and concerns. These conversations, which started about software, led to new faculty collaborations and cross-disciplinary work. Training and faculty development seminars about tech-nology and teaching did the same and they infused the campus with new and multiple cross-department conversations about teaching and learning.

As part of the change, the university developed new offices and pro-grams to support the rising technology needs of the campus. It created the ACE program "to bring students, faculty, staff and administrators to-gether to support the use of information technology to enhance teaching and learning." The program depends on trained undergraduates to provide faculty and academic departments with a range of services, including Web design, courseware, and hardware support. The university developed a technology and teaching resource component of its Center for Teaching Excellence. The university created a development fund for departments ($200,000) to support departmental infusion of technology into its major or general education courses. In addition, the development of a technol-ogy fellows program supports faculty-to-faculty innovation through course buy-out and stipends. The institution created a comprehensive assessment project "to study the long-term effects of technology on the campus learn-ing environment, and to ensure the quality of the mobile computing program." The institution thought differently about the new faculty it hired. No longer were scholarship and teaching the main criteria; the use of technology in those efforts became increasingly important in the search for junior faculty.

The institution has entered into new partnerships with software and hardware companies. It hosted national meetings on higher education, teaching, and computing, and it participated in national projects led by higher-education associations. The efforts on campus led to changes out-side the institution and in the ways the university interacts with its environment.

The ethos of the campus now focuses much more intentionally on undergraduate learning. Mobile computing coupled with innovations in residential life, a writing-across-the-curriculum project, and an institutional effort to lower the student-faculty ratio and create smaller classes has, as administrators and faculty both agree, changed the institution's culture. As one person noted, the new emphasis led by technology has "led faculty to ask fundamental questions about teaching and learning, and rethink teaching and learning."

Civic State University

A faculty leader at Civic State recently described its transformation process as moving the institution "characterized by instability, lack of identity, and both ignored by and ignoring its community to one that is recognized within the higher education community as a leader in comprehensive curricular reform, proud of its identity as an urban institution, and an integral component of its community." The transformation process at Civic State helped moved a nondescript regional university to one with a strong identity and a sense of self-confidence about its efforts to improve the community in which it is located.

Civic State's transformation efforts centered on a refocus of its mission to become an urban university. The hallmark of this transformation effort was a new integrative general education four-year curriculum. The first year, students participate in a yearlong interdisciplinary course sequence taught by the same professor. The second year, students choose three courses from different interdisciplinary clusters that act as a gateway to an upper-division set of courses. The latter courses, taken during the third year, "extend and develop one of the themes begun during sophomore year," allowing students to deepen their knowledge in an area of interest outside the major. The capstone experience, taken during the final year, is a six-credit interdisciplinary course built around a community-based project and intended to apply knowledge gained in the general education curriculum and the major.

This innovative general education program has catalyzed widespread change on campus. The general education program touches all students and by extension, all majors and departments. Even departments that traditionally do not have a strong presence in general education were offered opportunities to participate because of this program's interdisciplinary nature. Its interdisciplinary nature brought together faculty from various disciplines who had not previously worked together to plan, design, and implement the courses that make up the general education curriculum. The program draws on upper-class mentors to assist faculty teaching in the program, thereby creating a new relationship between students and faculty and reshaping ideas of who can teach. Because of concerns raised by some faculty over its effectiveness, the university developed a new assessment capacity to better understand student learning.

This general education program extended the idea of the classroom to the community and, in turn, led to new relationships and partnerships with community agencies, local business, and city government. Because the transformation agenda focused on the general education curriculum, the institution had to craft new policies and procedures for transfer students and form different relationships and agreements with local community colleges. The changes also led to new relationships with state policy makers. No longer was Civic State fighting its battle to be a research university in a state with a strong flagship university. As the university has articulated a new niche within the state and made changes to fulfill that mission, the state legislature has become more supportive. As it wrote in one report, "CSU is now in a situation in which it has forceful advocates and in which it can compete for public resources on more equal footing."

Because this approach challenged long-held assumptions of who can teach (by including student mentors), what topics departmental faculty can and should teach (because of its interdisciplinary focus), the academic calendar (by beginning with a three-term single course), and the integration of knowledge and practice (because the capstone was dependent on service learning), it generated significant conversation about teaching, learning, faculty roles, and the relationship between general education and the major. No longer could one go to faculty senate or departmental meetings without discussing these and related topics, creating a new tenor on campus. As one person noted, "The language of student learning is the point of departure for both supporters and critics of the curricular change."

The new general education program, coupled with other changes to emphasize the institution's emerging urban mission, led to the creation of a set of programs and initiatives that facilitated Civic State's transformation. The institution created a general education office and hired two long-time faculty members to lead it. It built and wired classrooms to support the new pedagogies of the general studies program. When the new unit was created, the provost moved the oversight responsibility and budget from the College of Letters and Sciences to the provost's office. The institution created the Center for Academic Excellence that, in addition to offering faculty development programs, facilitates community partnerships and coordinates campuswide assessment.

CONCLUSION

Transformation is a difficult type of change to bring about, as the varying progress among the twenty-three institutions in the project demonstrates. Issues such as time, institutional attention span, leadership turnover, uneven progress, and ever-changing environments work against easy transformation. For those institutions able to bring about transformation, the journey, as they realized, is never complete. Success only begets new challenges. Transformation is an important undertaking for the institution as it challenges culture, values, and priorities. It *should* be difficult; otherwise, the potential for instability could undermine much of the historic social and economic contributions colleges and universities make. American society might be ill served by colleges and universities wavering to each and every shift in the environment. The odds of successful transformation, as this project demonstrates, are against most institutions. However, institutions can and do succeed at transformation with significant dedication, institution-wide recognition and commitment, and a lot of hard work.

That said, even when institutions succeed at deep and pervasive change that alters cultures, there is not always consensus on campus that the transformation happened. As we define transformation, not everything will change, thus making it easy for some faculty to argue that from their departmental perspective, life is more similar than different. That response is to be expected because of different perspectives shaped by departmental realities, institutional structures that remain unchanged, and the continuance of the familiar activities of teaching, research, and service. The belief that meaningful change has not occurred may be even more predominant at large, complex institutions, not only because of their size but also because of the prevalence of strong departmental or college subcultures within the institution. When multiple subcultures exist, it is easy for the transformation to make the ideas, beliefs, and priorities of one subculture those of the institution. In these cases, although the institution has transformed, people from the units whose beliefs are now widespread may not realize that the rest of the institution has adopted its ways. For example, one faculty member at Civic State mentioned that not much in his department has changed. His department teaches mostly graduate students, who are not involved in the institution's innovative general education program. The nature of his discipline is service intensive, and his department has long had strong ties to the community. His courses and pedagogies have not changed drastically because "service learning" has always been an important component even before the higher education community labeled that approach. Much like a fish that does not recognize its environment is water, his departmental beliefs and norms have become mainstream, making it difficult for him to recognize that the rest of the institution is now swimming in his met-aphoric water.

NOTES

1. Much of this section is based on earlier versions that appear in the On Change Occasional Paper series produced by the American Council on Education.

2. Much of this section is based on the work of Eckel, Green, and Hill (2001).

CHAPTER 3

Helping People Think Differently

An Essential Element of Transformation

Transformation is as much about getting people to think differently as it is about anything else. Forging new collective understandings and creating new beliefs about institutional activities and people's roles are essential to transformation and, we found, more important than changing structures, creating reward incentives, aligning budgets, or making and implementing difficult decisions. A key part of transformation is changing mind-sets, which, in turn, alters behaviors, appreciations, commitments, and priorities. Over the course of transformation efforts, people develop new beliefs and interpretations and adopt new ways of thinking and perceiving that help create the foundation of significant change. Transformation is about making new sense. Without exploring what the changes mean for the institution and capturing the minds and hearts of faculty, staff, students, and trustees, institutional change will be limited to new organizational structures and policies that may not add up to transformation. In addition, these structural changes may very well conflict with the collective norms, assumptions, and expectations of the campus, resulting in little lasting change and possibly creating new problems. Change that occurs without altering the beliefs and assumptions about key elements, priorities, and processes will not be transformational.

ASKING "WHAT DOES THIS MEAN?"

The leaders at transforming colleges and universities asked their campuses questions about what the proposed changes would *mean* for the institution. They pushed their institutions to explore the implications for faculty work, pedagogies, budgets, and student support services, among others. For example, Sunshine Community College asked itself, "What does it mean for a community college to put learning first?" The question at the heart of the transformation efforts at Metropolitan University was, "What would be the implications for faculty in each discipline to take responsibility for all of the goals of general education?" At Midwest College, the president charged faculty to think about how becoming a socially responsible institution would affect the curriculum and cocurriculum, the role of staff in students' education, and student-faculty interactions. At Archdiocese University, the driving question was, "What are the implications for and potentials of putting a laptop computer in the hands of each and every student?" Each of these questions, and the others asked at Middle State University and Civic State, challenged faculty, administrators, staff, and often students to reexamine beliefs and assumptions and create new understandings, or what some organizational scholars call engaging in institutional "sensemaking" (Gioia & Chittipeddi, 1991; Weick, 1995).

We discovered that institutions forge two types of new understandings as part of the transformation process. First, colleges and universities attached new meanings to familiar concepts and ideas. Institutions, because they are not going to abandon their basic functions of teaching, research, and service, may develop new understandings for these terms (Duderstadt, 2000; Eckel, Hill, & Green, 1998). For example, while working on teaching and technology, Middle State University realized that through its change efforts, the idea of a "well-prepared professor" had evolved. No longer did it mean someone with well-organized lecture notes, clear outcomes for a course, and fair tests. It now meant someone who knew what technologically sophisticated tools were available within the discipline, when to use them, and for what purposes. The "well-prepared professor," as one person explained, now "knew where the keys to the computer cabinet were and how to use the stuff inside." Because of their important social missions, colleges and universities will retain most of their objectives and structures even during times of transformation (Salipante & Golden-Biddle, 1995), suggesting that a rethinking, rather than a discarding, of their fundamental aspects is likely to occur.

Second, the transforming institutions developed new languages and adopted new concepts to describe the changed institution. For example, Sunshine Community College added well-defined words such as *customer* and *client* to its collective vocabulary. Once a faculty leader started talking about "customers," other campus leaders knew that individual was referring to companies that hired their graduates, local businesses that contracted for educational and training programs for their employees, and local and state elected officials. When the campus spoke about its "clients," it was referring to students, both degree and nondegree seeking. They collectively decided to adopt the term *clients* to stress the nature of the relationship they were trying to create with their students, seeing them as individuals with particular needs—sometimes well defined, other times not so much—who made a conscious decision to attend the college, as they have other convenient choices for their education.

Collective understanding plays important roles in the life of any college or university. Although we try to make our institutions as rational as possible, the complexities and ambiguity associated with organizational life make that difficult (Birnbaum, 1988; March, 1994). Colleges and universities are "full of problems that cannot be answered, problems that cannot be solved, and events that cannot be understood or managed" (Bolman & Deal, 1991, p. 253). To compensate for the uncertainties, people work to understand collectively what is occurring by interpreting ambiguous events and assigning them meaning. For example, the act of hiring a director to launch a new undergraduate honors program does not by itself have much meaning. For an institution trying to recruit and retain more academically talented students, this act most likely will be interpreted as desirable and an important step to realize an institutional commitment. On the other hand, for an institution trying to retain more students who are dropping out, hiring this person over what is perceived to be much-needed academic support staff or tutors may be interpreted as riding roughshod over what were thought to be important institutional goals and an act inconsistent with what were thought to be agreed-upon priorities. Faculty, trustees, and legislators could easily perceive this act as one of administrative defiance. Organizational life is messy and uncertain, and people continually work to make it more easily understood and straightforward.

People have to work to understand not only what events mean but also what problems should get their attention. In the busy mix of institutional life, problem identification is as much work as problem solving. Schon (1983) describes this constant clarification process:

In real-world practice, problems do not present themselves to the practitioner as givens. They must be constructed from the materials of problematic situations, which are puzzling, troubling, and uncertain. . . . When we set the problem, we select what we will treat as the "things" of the situation, we set the boundaries of our attention to it, and we impose upon it a coherence which allows us to say what is wrong and in what direction the situation needs to be changed. Problem setting is a process in which, interactively, we *name* the things to which we will attend and *frame* the context in which we will attend to them. (p. 40)

Institutions thus engage in ongoing processes to understand the complexities and nuances of the world in which they function. Without an agreement on what things mean, institutions would be unable to function because they would continually face what appear to be random, conflicting, and meaningless events (Birnbaum, 1988). A constant implicit negotiation occurs over what things mean to create a shared interpretation that provides a basis on which to set priorities and act. There are many plausible ways in which the environment can be experienced and events can be interpreted. Institutions create a subjective reality by continually negotiating meaning and trying to reach a consistent understanding. During times of transformation, this process occurs more frequently, and its outcomes (new beliefs and understandings) become more important to understanding the shifting terrain.

In this chapter, we explore the institutional sensemaking processes that are essential to transformation. We learned that beliefs and mind-sets must change, as well as behaviors and structures, if transformation is to occur. Changing structures and priorities without changing perceptions and understandings may only lead to short-term results. As Schein (1992) notes in his work on cultural change, "Behavior change can be coerced, but it will not last once the coercive force is lifted unless cognitive redefinition has preceded or accompanied it" (p. 302). Helping people think differently is the process that brings about the cognitive redefinition necessary throughout the institution.

Why did we determine that sensemaking or making people think differently was so important to transformational change? After reviewing the stories of campuses that made the most progress toward transformation, we found that they had used five core strategies, which are presented in Chapter 4. We asked ourselves if there was anything common about these five strategies and deduced that they were each ways that campuses helped people to think differently. Thus, sensemaking has become an underlying and essential element of all campuses' efforts to transform. In the next chapter, we review the core strategies and highlight how they each helped members of campus communities to make new sense and to rethink the way things are done.

NEW UNDERSTANDINGS AND TRANSFORMATION

Transformational change, as defined here, alters organizational structures and processes, leads to reorganized priorities, affects organizational assumptions and ideologies, and is a collective, institution-wide undertaking. Familiar and long-standing meanings and interpretations—which compose the current negotiated reality—are challenged as the circumstances in which the institution finds itself change. Change of this magnitude creates an uncertainty that asks for a collective interpretation of three key questions: "what is 'out there,' what is 'in here,' and who must we be in order to deal with those questions?" (Weick, 1995, p. 70). Institutions undertake a process, often implicitly, that helps to answer those questions (Bartunek, 1984; Smircich, 1983).

Developing new understandings is frequently initiated by a realization that old interpretations no longer suffice, which frequently takes the form of a shock when people reach a threshold of dissatisfaction (Starbuck & Milliken, 1988; Weick, 1995). This dissatisfaction helps bring issues into focus that may have been part of the background of the indiscernible environment and helps people to see things differently. Thus, developing a new collective understanding begins with an acknowledgment that something is amiss. In times of transformation, leaders may provide the rationale and evidence that change is necessary for the institution, calling attention to issues that heighten collective dissatisfaction.

An organizational theorist (Weick, 1995) postulates that developing new collective understandings (what he calls "institutional sensemaking") has seven properties that can be a template to identifying change process activities that help to forge new collective understandings: (1) forging new understanding starts with identity; (2) it occurs retrospectively; (3) it depends on interpretations of the environment; (4) it is social; (5) it is ongoing; (6) it builds on points of reference that emerge and cumulate over time; and (7) plausibility, not accuracy, is important to collective new understanding.

Understanding Starts with Identity

To develop a common meaning from the ambiguity associated with change, people begin from their own roles and identities. How people perceive themselves shapes the sense made. Who one is as a faculty member, student, administrator, or trustee shapes the inferences drawn and the understanding developed. For example, two groups of faculty who define their roles differently will draw different conclusions about the provost's new effort to improve undergraduate education. Those who define their primary roles as generating new knowledge might see the new emphasis as a challenge to their sense of self and in response, may resist the efforts. Faculty who define their roles as primarily teachers might perceive this campus effort as reassuring and thus act favorably toward it. The ways in which people interpret their roles shape the meaning they make. During periods of uncertainty, people ask themselves continuously, "What implications do these events have for who I will be?" (Weick, 1995, pp. 23–24).

Understanding Comes Retrospectively

People can only understand what has already occurred. Only upon reflection can people figure out what that event, activity, or incident meant as it stands in comparison to other events about which they understand. "Actions are known only when they have been completed, which means we are always a little behind or our actions are always a bit ahead of us" (Weick, 1995, p. 26). For example, categorizing an emerging issue as either a threat or an opportunity depends on past understandings. For one institution, the opening of a new community college in a nearby town came to be viewed as an opportunity, not a threat. The campus realized that, yes, it would lose students to the community college. However, it came to understand collectively that the community college would allow the institution to spend more time and energy recruiting better-prepared students and that it could partner with the community college to meet the needs of lesser-prepared students that it had traditionally been fighting to serve on its own. Other institutions may have interpreted the opening of the community college as a threat.

Interpretations Shape Understanding

The environment is full of incidents that in and of themselves do not have any one meaning and that ask to be collectively understood. In most cases, the environment itself is open to negotiation and is shaped by those seeking to understand it. Rarely is the environment itself a static, knowable entity. "People create their environments as those environments create them" (Weick, 1995, p. 34). It is widely accepted that the environment shapes institutional activities and priorities. For instance, institutions create new degree programs to meet emerging needs. However, just as computer companies created markets for the personal computer when none existed, the activities of institutions shape and influence their external environments, creating an interaction effect. For example, when the University of Phoenix offers courses in a new city, it alters the higher education environment. However, the types of programs the University of Phoenix offers frequently are shaped by those offered by the original institution. Thus, while the environment is being understood, by the process of understanding it alters the environment. The process is trying to name a moving target as the institution and the environment are acting, interacting, and reacting to one another.

Understanding Is a Social Process

Creating new institution-wide understandings is done through talk, discourse, and conversation and is based on interaction. The nature of work in organizations is social. People understand that their activities and decisions will be completed in "the presence of others or with the knowledge that they will have to be implemented, or understood, or approved by others" (Burns & Stalker, 1961, as cited in Weick, 1995). They together develop a "common language" that shapes what they think and perceive.

Understanding is shaped by shared experiences, not just meaning and language. For example, participating in the same meeting helps catalyze meaning by providing a foundation from which people can negotiate meaning: What was it about that meeting that led us to think the same or differently about it? What defines a productive meeting, if we agree that this one wasn't, although for different reasons? Creating a common understanding depends on the interactions of people working together, obtaining information from one another, acting, and reacting.

Creating Collective Understanding Is Ongoing

The process of developing new meaning has no beginning, middle, or end; new sense is made continuously. However, understanding depends on the ways in which people "chop moments out of the continuous flows and extract cues from those moments" (Weick, 1995, p. 43). When the "everyday-ness" of life is interrupted, people become more aware of the typically invisible routines of activities, meanings, and events, and of their disruptions. Disruptions call current beliefs and understandings into question and ask for new perspectives, responses, and meanings. The disruptions—such as the release of a major academic senate task force report, the hiring of a new dean, or the retirement of a valuable faculty member—jolt people into recognizing that the event is special. These activities, as

Eccles and Nohria (1992) note, "focus and crystallize meanings in organizations. . . . Although they may often only be ceremonial and not be
remembered as events of any significance, they serve as moments to take
stock of ongoing actions, to spin new stories, to set in motion future
actions, to formally announce beginnings, milestones, and ends, to trigger
a change of course, or just to touch base and reaffirm individual and
organizational identities" (p. 48).

Forging New Understandings Requires Reference Points

The ongoing activities and disruptions provide points of reference that
capture people's attention and ask that meaning be made. These elements
are the building blocks of sensemaking. Independently, each may have
little effect, but they add up over time and through experience to challenge existing beliefs and understandings. These cues become associated
not only with one another but also with more general notions used to
clarify the meaning of a particular experience or phenomenon. Like
weights on a scale, eventually enough cues are built up over time to tip
understanding in a new direction.

Creating New Understandings Is Driven by Plausibility, Not Accuracy

Accuracy is nice but not necessary to create new understandings (Weick,
1995). More important is plausibility. Collective understanding is not
about being right; rather, it is about being acceptable, coherent, reason-
able, credible, and pragmatic. As previously discussed, organizations are
full of complex and ambiguous events that in and of themselves do not
have specific meaning. Finding the right understanding for each event is
not as important as creating a plausible one. People respond not because
something is proven true but because the explanation seems plausible
(Weick, 1995). Because objects in the environment have the potential
for multiple meanings, a single explanation (or truth) rarely exists; so
when explanations seem credible, we accept them as so. For organizations
to function, it is more critical to get *an* interpretation rather than the
exact one.

In fact, inaccuracy, misperceptions, errors, and mistakes are part of life
in complex organizations and may contribute to an institution's effectiveness rather than detract from it. As Sutcliffe (1994) notes, "[B]ecause
environments aren't seen accurately, managers may undertake potentially
difficult courses of action with enthusiasm, effort, and self-confidence

necessary to bring about success. Having an accurate environmental map may be less important than having some map that brings order to the world and prompts action" (p. 1374).

This chapter concentrates on the activities and tools associated with sensemaking because they are the common denominator of the core strategies essential to transformational change. We use Weick's seven properties to identify the tools that shape the creation and adoption of new understandings related to institutional transformation. What people *do* contributes to new understandings and meanings (Weick, 1995). Thus, in times of change, strategies and activities help new meanings become assigned to organization activities and events (Gioia, Thomas, Clark, & Chittipeddi, 1996). The next section identifies activities that helped transforming institutions develop new understandings.

CREATING NEW UNDERSTANDINGS

Through this chapter, we explore the processes and activities that facilitate new collective understandings at transforming colleges and universities and what leaders can do to facilitate this as part of the change process. The institutions, we discovered, (1) were engaged in inclusive, ongoing, and widespread conversations that built upon one another, (2) developed inclusive processes to articulate and develop a set of concrete and meaningful concepts, (3) used cross-departmental working groups, (4) gave public presentations, (5) created faculty and staff development opportunities, including new faculty socialization experiences, and (6) benefited from outsiders and their ideas.

For three institutions—Sunshine Community College, Civic State University, and Midwest College—we first describe the predominant old and new sense. We then briefly describe key elements that contributed to sensemaking. The activities and events for each are organized in roughly chronological order.

Sunshine Community College

Before its efforts, one of the central dominant beliefs at Sunshine Community College was that teaching was the most important activity. Through the ensuing transformation efforts, the college moved toward the understanding that learning, not teaching, is the centerpiece of its core function. Another shift was from one in which administrators know best regarding making institutional decisions to an inclusive and open

process in which the best decisions are made through widespread collaboration. Associated with the adoption of collaborative decision making was an abandonment of the idea that good decisions were made
quickly. The college redefined its definition of good decision making to
include the outcomes and implementation of ideas and widespread collaboration with faculty, not the speed with which decisions were made.
As one report noted, "The culture in 1995 was one in which we like to
act quickly, seek outside assistance, value what is logical, emphasize the
objective and drive toward decisions. We would likely have had as a
motto, 'Fish or cut bait.' We have learned that such an organization must
make a conscious effort to slow down and take the time to communicate
and collaborate." Associated with this change was a new belief that faculty were interested in the college beyond simply the classroom. The
college also changed from a shared perspective in which "students were
to be processed" to one in which "students were to be developed." Finally,
the definition of a good faculty member changed from one of "solo flyer"
to "team member" as the college adopted a collaborative ethos not only
in decision making but in the teaching and learning process.

Sunshine Community College engaged in the following activities to
facilitate its change efforts that likely contributed to the new collective
understandings.

1996 Roundtable Conversations

The administrative and faculty team responsible for the learning-centered
initiative sponsored a series of twelve roundtable conversations from May
through September. They invited all full-time faculty and staff, and approximately three hundred participated. The invitation letter announced:
"We know that there are many ways to describe a learning-centered institution and to focus on student achievement. How can we at [Sunshine]
arrive at our own unique definition and move toward realizing it?" These
conversations of twenty to thirty people each focused on understanding
the changing local environment and on "developing consensus on a definition of a learning-centered college and defining action steps, including
a set of student core competencies, analyzing the college's core processes,
and exploring learning and curriculum theory and design issues." Campus
change leaders compiled and circulated collegewide summaries of the
conversations as a follow-up activity. They asked all faculty and staff to
comment on the summaries. Based on the documents and the comments,
the leadership team developed a draft definition of a learning-centered
college.

Transformation Workshop

The month following the final roundtable, the leadership team sponsored a workshop for administrators and key faculty and staff leaders to discuss concepts and ideas of change and transformation, review the outcomes of the roundtable conversations, and craft recommendations for moving forward. The primary recommendation was to create a set of action teams.

January Roundtable and Action Teams

At the beginning of the winter semester, the campus held a new series of collegewide roundtables to introduce the concepts and language of change, discuss the implications for the college of becoming learning-centered, and invite membership on action teams. Approximately 170 people participated in this open-invitation meeting. Participants were divided into small groups and were invited to discuss the documents created to date, including the draft definition of a learning-centered college. They also discussed how best to proceed. Following the January meeting, four action teams of faculty, staff, and administrator volunteers began their work: Short-Term Action Team; Vision and Organizational Character Action Team; Core Processes Action Team; and Core Competencies Action Team. Members of the action teams were volunteers who selected their own leaders.

The college has since developed a second set of action teams. These cross-campus groups of faculty, administrators, and staff include a developmental advising action team, a curriculum design action team, and a learning theory action team.

Welcome Back Retreat

The following August, after the first action teams completed their work, the campus held a welcome back retreat, attended by more than three hundred people. The purpose of the retreat was to present the work of the action teams and consider their recommendations. The three hundred people attending were separated into smaller groups. Each group saw a videotape of the four teams' presentations. Participants received written reports as well. Retreat participants commented on draft documents of the student core competencies, the campus vision statement, and the proposed core processes model. Participants were asked to discuss how they, as individuals, currently contributed to students' core competencies and to student learning. They were asked to consider the proposed core competencies in light of their own work at the college. From the discussions, the student core competencies became articulated in four words—Think, Act, Communicate, Value—with a description of learning outcomes for each.

Faculty and Staff Development

In fall 1997, the college launched a comprehensive set of leadership development activities for all faculty, administrators, and staff. Many of these activities and workshops were aligned with the emerging change agenda. The work of the action teams shaped the agendas of many of the workshops. Individuals who participated in these activities were given opportunities to link the new ways of thinking and operating of the ongoing changes to their own activities. College leaders sponsored optional annual summer workshops on teaching underprepared students. They also offered a retreat focusing on teaching and learning for all new full-time faculty at the college. The college initiated a series of discipline-based conversations across the four college campuses, inviting faculty teaching the same discipline to discuss "what might be done to enhance learning in that discipline," with a particular focus on pedagogical strategies and student success. This effort was the first time that the college had attempted to facilitate faculty conversations about teaching and learning across the four colleges.

Reference Guide and Other Documents

As a tool to "foster dialogue and ensure clearer communication," change leaders developed the *Learning-Centered Reference Guide,* a small, laminated handbook of relevant terms, definitions, ideas, and additional resources associated with learning. The change leaders noted, "We found it helpful to develop a shared vocabulary that enabled us to talk about change and the values we hold dear. . . . When external reviewers have visited the college, they comment on the careful use of language and on the shared meaning." College leaders also developed draft statements of a learning-centered college, of their core competencies, of their core processes. They had begun to identify all documents as "drafts"; realizing that the documents would evolve as their learning grew, they wanted to send a message of flexibility and a willingness to reconsider and change.

Presentations and Other Activities

College faculty and administrators engaged concurrently in other activities throughout the change process. These included giving numerous presentations and workshops at national conferences (e.g., the American Association for Higher Education (AAHE) and the League for Innovation) and an on-campus project that involved clusters of faculty meeting together who teach courses with shared enrollments (the Linkages Project). The college also secured over $3.75 million in external grants to assist faculty to integrate the core competencies throughout the curriculum and assess their results.

Civic State University

Civic State, through its transformation efforts, developed a new collective mind-set about the importance of community as a contributor to students' education and as a recipient of the institution's work and graduates. Prior to the changes, the institution viewed the community as something to be ignored and as having little to contribute to the institution outside of taxpayer dollars. As part of its change process, the university adopted a more open and inclusive view of the community as an important resource for its scholarship and teaching activities, and as a place in which to form meaningful partnerships. Civic State also developed a different perspective on the role of faculty: it moved from the dominant sense that faculty disseminate information and test for comprehension to new beliefs that redefined faculty roles much more complexly. The shared sense now is that good faculty not only provide content knowledge and test but also facilitate learning and are themselves learners in the process of teaching and thus are important role models for students as learners.

Civic State also adopted a new sense about who is responsible for student learning. It redefined this concept to include librarians, technology resource people, other students as peer mentors, and student affairs professionals. The notion of the ideal student also changed. It went from students who were attentive in class (and showed up) to students who were active participants in control of their own learning and discovery. This shift was a difficult one for some faculty and students. Many students did not want this added responsibility or to expend energy in this new way, and some faculty saw the no-longer-passive students as "uppity" (a descriptor we learned that was widely known) and difficult. The institution also redefined learning to mean not only content mastery but discovery, translation, and application. Finally, Civic State is in the midst of making new sense about "valuable information" to be delivered in the classroom. The institution is moving toward a cross-disciplinary (not interdisciplinary) mind-set and away from disciplinary silos.

Civic State engaged in the following activities to facilitate its change efforts that contributed to these new collective understandings.

Campus Seminar

This institution adopted what its faculty and administrators called a "scholarly approach to change," which resulted in a series of campus seminars for interested faculty and administrators. Organized by the provost, the first seminar included "an historical, sociological, and economic examination of the academy, with a specific focus on the development and challenges of the urban university." The provost identified an initial set of readings to focus discussion. In the first seminar, eighteen faculty and administrators participated, meeting monthly to discuss assigned readings.

Symposium

Those participating in the first seminar organized a campus symposium on the "changing faculty roles and work" in the fall of 1996. Titled *Faculty Time: Chaos, Crisis and Continuity*, the symposium brought together close to two hundred faculty and staff. The morning consisted of plenary sessions featuring campus administrators and national experts. The afternoon consisted of responses by faculty leaders and a series of small group conversations to allow more faculty to "consider the issues and make recommendations."

Seminars Continued and Extended

Following the symposium, participants in the seminar reviewed the remarks and comments from symposium conversations. They identified five themes—technology, new definitions of scholarship, faculty responsibility for curricular design and student success, integration of academic support personnel and instructional staff, and enhancing community—and created working groups for each. Each of these groups recruited additional faculty members to participate. They developed a reading list and questions to focus their inquiry. Each team then sponsored a set of campus conversations to further explore the issues and involve more faculty in their conversations.

Center for Academic Excellence

The institution concurrently developed its Center for Academic Excellence (CAE) into a comprehensive campus resource. The center's three-fold mission is to enhance teaching and improve student learning outcomes, to establish community-university partnerships that are "central to the fulfillment of the institution's urban mission," and to support assessment of academic programs and instruction. The CAE offers a range of services and programs, including workshops for department chairs, a mentor program for junior faculty, a range of seminars on teaching, learning, assessment, and community-based learning, and workshops on the scholarship of teaching. It launched a brown-bag series for faculty to talk informally about teaching. The center has facilitated more than one hundred new community-based learning courses. The CAE sponsors a "Focus on Faculty Day" to kick off the academic year, which includes mini-workshops and discussions on a range of topics associated with teaching and learning. It also runs an orientation for new faculty.

Cross-Campus Working Groups

Administrators have organized a group of cross-departmental working groups. These groups have focused on topics such as developing the CAE, supporting community-university partnerships, improving campus assessment, setting new promotion and tenure guidelines consistent with emerging institutional goals and purposes, and developing a set of recommendations on campus climate. The most visible working group is the one working to create and implement the new general education curriculum.

National Conversation

Campus leaders involved the institution in many national conversations and projects (beyond the ACE project). Faculty and staff were encouraged (and funded) to present sessions and workshops at the Association of American Colleges and Universities (AAC&U) and AAHE, among other conferences, and to participate in the Urban University Portfolio Project, the Quality Assurance at Urban Public Comprehensive Universities Project, and the Kellogg Network on Institutional Transformation. As one administrator noted, "The national discussion regarding issues and problems in higher education sustains the change. Faculty exposure to and participation in this discussion increases their [the faculty's] interest and understanding of our change process."

One result of active participation in national dialogues and projects was an influx of visitors to the institution. These visits have forced faculty and administrators to articulate what they are doing and why, and to refine their ideas. As one person commented, "Even faculty who don't want anything to do with this [new general education curriculum] cannot avoid people coming here and asking questions."

Midwest College

Similar to Civic State, Midwest College redefined "what constitutes a learning opportunity and who facilitates student learning." No longer are faculty viewed as the only educators on campus. This responsibility has been extended to student affairs professionals. Midwest also now widely believes that valuable learning occurs not only in the classroom but outside it as well, particularly through service-learning and community engagement. The college has also adopted a new perspective that learning is not solely about knowledge acquisition but that it must also be used ultimately for individual and social responsibility. They have added a new dimension to learning, the ends to which it serves. The role of students has also shifted from one of passive recipient of material to one in which they must take responsibility not only for learning material but also for assessing and charting their intellectual development and growth. As one person put it, students have become "agents of their own learning." Assessment, particularly through student learning portfolios, has become part and parcel of the learning experience at the college.

Midwest College engaged in the following activities to forge these collective understandings.

Labor Day Forum

In September 1993, the newly hired president convened a campus forum to issue a challenge to the faculty: "Given all the options that are available to students in terms of their choice of a college, why should anyone want to come to [Midwest]?" The charge was to recraft the college's mission and core purposes, keeping in mind the history of the institution, academic distinctiveness, diversity, community, fiscal integrity, and operating effectiveness. The outcome of this forum was a Vision Commission of faculty volunteers who took the responsibility for developing a process to create a new vision statement for the college. To draft the vision, the commission engaged in widespread conversation with faculty, staff, administrators, and students, floating ideas and seeking input and feedback. The Vision Commission drew heavily on the college's founding ideals and created a new vision focused on social purpose and civic commitments.

Faculty Forum and Board Approval

That December, the Vision Commission released its draft document at a second collegewide forum. During the December forum, faculty discussed and debated the vision statement and its appropriateness for the college. At the end of the day, 88 percent of the faculty voted to accept it.

Learning Outcomes Group

After gaining unanimous board approval for the new vision statement, the president asked the faculty to explore the implications of the newly adopted vision statement for student learning. Faculty formed an informal Learning Outcomes Group. All faculty were invited to participate. A group of faculty worked to articulate the learning outcomes. At a special faculty meeting in February, the faculty debated and voted on the proposed outcomes. Some items were modified, and at the end of the meeting, 84 percent of the faculty accepted the proposed student outcomes.

Four Working Groups

In March 1994, the president held a third faculty forum asking the faculty to develop a new academic program to deliver the agreed-upon learning outcomes. He suggested creating four working groups to collect information about various innovative undergraduate curriculums. Each working group was to conduct site visits over the summer and bring back different models and ideas about how the college might best deliver its education for civic responsibility. Twenty-four faculty volunteered to participate.

The following Labor Day (1994), the four working groups presented their findings. Each of the four models offered was supported equally. After intense debate among the faculty and administrators who led the working groups, the president and the leadership crafted a model that incorporated elements from each model. This new model fully embraced the belief that students learn from the full range of their experiences. Campus leaders presented the new plan to the faculty, of which 90 percent supported its adoption. The new model was later named the Midwest Design.

Task Forces

The college organized eight different task forces, each responsible for implementing a different element of the new academic plan. Faculty volunteered to participate in the task forces. A collegewide Implementation

Team composed of faculty and administrators coordinated the activities across the task forces. Each task force included faculty from a range of departments. One faculty participant noted that "there were a lot of them [task forces] and a lot of us on them. They estimated that 50%–60% of the faculty have been involved and report that [the effect has been] 'the faculty have become empowered.' "

Creating the Compact

In April 1997, the campus held a retreat open to all college employees, students, and trustees. This open dialogue was created for the college to "articulate its most basic values" and "begin an inclusive process to give further definition to the institutional vision. The goal was to formulate a set of principles about what it means to be a responsible member of the college community." More than 250 people attended, meeting in the college gymnasium. Originally framed as a set of principles for students, the conversation was enlarged to include responsibilities of all college community members.

Following the retreat, draft documents were circulated, debated, and refined through ongoing conversations across campus. By the end of the spring semester, the document, called the College Compact, was formally endorsed by the student and staff senates, by the entire faculty, and by the board of trustees.

The College Compact became a set of guiding principles for continued changes. For example, it is being used as a guide for student conduct hearings, to frame the Freshmen Year Experience course, and to formulate new policies for the Greek-letter student societies. A bronzed copy of the compact hangs in the hallway of the administration building.

External Support and Engagement

Throughout the college's efforts, leaders involved the college and its faculty in multiple national projects. Faculty participated in networks with other institutions, where they discussed the challenges they were facing, gained new ideas to shape their ongoing efforts, and explored ideas in a low-risk environment. Campus leaders wrote grant applications describing the aspirations and progress of the institution's transformation. From these applications, the college secured multiple grants from local and national foundations. The college created a relationship with Stephen Covey's Institute for Principle-Centered Leadership and with state and local civic organizations. The entire campus community participated in a two-day workshop on Covey's Seven Habits of Highly Effective People.

Public Documents

The college produced a series of documents to communicate its efforts. It rewrote the campus handbook to reflect the new vision and compact. It developed a publication, called *Midwest Notes*, primarily sent to external audiences, describing the successes to date and conveying challenges facing the college.

Experts

The college drew on nationally known consultants to help implement its vision and the new academic plan, and to develop a strategy to assess student learning outcomes. It also created a speaker series bringing to campus local, national, and international speakers including church and civic leaders, social activists, writers, and government officials who could address issues of civic responsibility and the social role of the university.

TOOLS FOR NEW UNDERSTANDINGS

The following strategies surfaced as important to helping institutions think differently as part of transformational change. To highlight the connections of each to sensemaking, we italicize elements that reflect Weick's sensemaking framework.

Different institutional sizes, structures, and cultures suggest some distinctions between approaches (explored further in chapter 6); however, similar approaches emerged across these three institutions that suggest a cluster of strategies. One set—engaging in continuous, widespread conversations, developing cross-departmental teams and working groups, benefiting from outsiders and their ideas, and sponsoring faculty and staff development opportunities—occurred at the beginning and middle of their efforts. At later stages, the activities switched to preparing and giving public presentations and creating documents or concrete sets of ideas. This evolution of time does not suggest that institutions stopped their other activities, although the proportion of time and attention spent on them changed.

Numerous, Continuous, and
Widespread Conversations

Ongoing and widespread campus conversations played important roles in helping these institutions adopt new mental models and create new collective understandings. These conversations allowed people to recast key concepts to fit new realities and to explore the ways in which they fit into the emerging future. Through conversations held at retreats, seminars, roundtables, and symposia, faculty, staff, and administrators developed a new common language and a consensus on ideas, which helped to reframe key core concepts. These conversations allowed people to explore different conceptions of key issues; for example, what is a learning-centered institution at Sunshine, or what does it mean to be an urban university at Civic State? They created opportunities for people to think about the ways in which the changes might impact their duties and responsibilities. For example, at Midwest, what will it mean to me as a faculty member to be socially responsible as stated in the College Compact? Change leaders framed these conversations to clarify and explore new concepts and ideas and to test assumptions, rather than to advance or argue positions.

These conversations were multiple and ongoing. Leaders at each of the three institutions created multiple opportunities for participants to collectively wrestle with ideas and new ways of thinking. Each institution held sets of roundtables, retreats, meetings, and symposia. In addition, the conversations were continued over a series of gatherings. Each conversation built upon the preceding one; no conversation stood alone. A one-time conversation was insufficient to work through issues as difficult and complex as creating new cognitive frameworks. This process would not occur in a short two-hour meeting or even a single daylong roundtable.

The conversations were inclusive and widespread. All three institutions used open invitations and included many members of the campus community—upwards of three hundred people at Sunshine, two hundred people at Civic State, and most faculty and other community members at Midwest. All were invited, and the convenors intentionally designed them to accommodate large groups of people, be it in the gymnasium (Midwest) or through coordinated roundtables using common videotaped presentations to provide the same context in each room (Sunshine). These roundtables, symposia, and retreats were held at the beginning of the academic semester or on the weekend to ensure maximum participation. (We would also guess that they fed people, although our data do not provide that level of detail.)

The conversations allowed people to construct *new identities* collaboratively and openly (i.e., they were *social*). In many cases, they were *retrospective* in that they discussed what was unfolding in light of events that had occurred or in comparison with past beliefs and activities. They frequently started from commentaries on the *changing environment*. They focused on particular elements of the change process and often concerned what is *plausible* for the institution given its history, norms, and social functions.

Cross-Departmental Teams

All three institutions implemented cross-departmental work teams. These teams brought together different combinations of faculty, administrators, and staff (and occasionally, students) from across the institution who had different perspectives and different assumptions. Many institutions conduct their work through departmental "silos," with little cross-unit interaction. The tasks these teams were charged with and their interactions and collective explorations most likely led to discussions about beliefs, assumptions, and ideas. The cross-fertilization of ideas and the challenges associated with bringing together people with diverse perspectives helped to encourage the exchange of ideas that led to new understandings.

These teams were *social*, in that they brought together people to work on a set of concrete tasks. They touched upon *identity* as ideas were tested to determine their fit with the institution and its goals. Team members discussed what was realistic *(plausible)* and likely for the institution. They focused on smaller components *(cues)* of the comprehensive change agenda that provided the "seeds" for making new meaning. They were *ongoing*; teams met many times to continue previous conversations. It is difficult to tell the extent to which cross-departmental groups discussed the environment and were retrospective.

Faculty and Staff Training

Sunshine Community College and Civic State both developed comprehensive faculty development programs to support their change agendas. They offered a wide range of programs to meet the diverse needs of faculty. However, most of their efforts were aligned with the direction of the change agenda. For example, within the long list of activities sponsored by Civic State's Center for Academic Excellence, many faculty could find something of interest. The framework shaping the workshops was the urban university, thus exposing the ideas and notions to a range of faculty participants. In addition, both these groups offered orientation programs for new faculty, helping to influence their socialization into the institution.

Although little formal faculty and staff development occurred at Midwest beyond the Seven Habits seminars, one could speculate that the institution's small size might have limited formal on-campus faculty development. The prevalence of the College Compact may have influenced new faculty socialization in ways similar to a formal orientation. Participating in national projects, interacting with grant funders, and visiting other institutions may have provided nontraditional faculty development opportunities.

Faculty and staff development opportunities brought together people in a *social* way to learn new skills and gain new knowledge related to the unfolding changes. Some of these activities were *ongoing* and included brown-bag discussions, seminars, and faculty discussion groups. They focused on small elements (such as seminars on using portfolio assessment or creating community-based learning experiences) that would contribute to larger, institutional goals. They focused on adapting ideas from elsewhere (portfolio assessment) and making them *plausible* to fit local contexts and challenges.

Outsiders and Their Ideas

The change processes at these three institutions benefited from the ideas, comments, suggestions, and challenges from interested outsiders. These outsiders challenged key institutional beliefs and assumptions. In many instances, they, particularly if they were invited speakers or paid consultants, had latitude to ask challenging questions that would be difficult for campus leaders to raise. Sometimes, institutions invited outside speakers to participate in campus retreats. Midwest sponsored a lecture series with a list of speakers who raised questions and brought new ideas related to the change agenda.

The institutions also benefited by sending faculty and administrators to off-campus activities. The president of Midwest sponsored four teams to visit other institutions to collect new ideas about various delivery systems. All the institutions participated in a variety of national projects. They also sent groups of faculty and administrators to regional and national conferences.

Leaders at all three institutions widely distributed key readings and developed ways to discuss those readings at retreats, during regularly scheduled meetings, or through reading groups specifically organized as professional seminars. In all cases, leaders did not simply distribute readings; they developed mechanisms to actively engage the campus in a discussion of those ideas presented.

Outsiders and their ideas reached groups of people, and their writings and ideas were actively discussed by many. They challenged old ways of knowing and perceiving, helping the institution to consider what is *plausible* and to reflect *collectively* on past ways of operating and thinking. They provided *cues* and brought perspectives on the *changing environment*. The influence of outsiders may not have been ongoing, except where institutions used readings as part of continuing faculty development opportunities.

Creating Defining Documents

Change leaders organized processes to develop a guiding document (or set of documents) or to articulate a set of concrete ideas that would shape the direction of the change agenda and connect it to important institutional values. Examples include the general education curriculum at Civic State, the College Compact vision and plan at Midwest, and the ideas Act, Value, Think, Communicate and the draft definition of a more learning-centered college at Sunshine.

Although the documents themselves often made important contributions, the process of creating, drafting, circulating, discussing, rewriting, presenting, and polishing the document may have been the larger contribution to redefining key ideas related to the change agenda. The process of writing down important ideas got people to talk about their assumptions, engaged them continuously and deeply, and tapped into their abilities and strengths as scholars. For example, look to the iterative processes at Sunshine to draft the statement of its core competencies for students. To create this document, change leaders sponsored a set of campuswide discussions that led to a draft statement. This statement was, in turn, discussed at subsequent faculty retreats, in cabinet meetings and at campuswide forums, which resulted in modifications to the document. The leaders subsequently asked the campus for additional written comments.

The process of creating documents and developing concrete ideas involved many people (*social*). At none of the institutions did a single person draft a document alone. These documents discussed what the institution was becoming, thus acknowledging past ways of operating (*retrospective*). The content typically addressed institutional *identity* and focused on key elements of the new institutional mental models. The documents tended to be inward focused and did not discuss the environment, except in prefatory comments.

Public Presentations

The institutions created numerous opportunities for a variety of people involved in the change efforts to give public presentations about the institution and its change agenda. The practicality of putting together and delivering presentations may have helped unfreeze mental frames and begin to develop new models. First, organizing a presentation for public consumption demands that people think about their ideas and assumptions. Second, hearing their own presentations and speaking aloud create another opportunity for an individual or group to catalyze thoughts. Finally, the presenters have an opportunity to hear and respond to questions from the audience. Over time, the cumulative effect may have been that their thinking became more clear and their ideas more concrete.

The process of putting together public comments was rarely a solo activity (*social*). The public presentations tended to focus on what the institution had become or had accomplished and, thus, was *retrospective*. It reinforced what was *plausible* within the institution's culture and built upon ongoing work, ideas, and accomplishments. These presentations told audience members who the institution was, what it was becoming, and why. They brought together discrete elements of the change process and placed them in a larger perspective. Because these presentations showcased institutional activities, the connection to the environment was not always evident.

Making the Case for Change

Through the activities that helped institutions redefine understandings and create new meanings, we can see that leaders were intentional about making a clear and compelling case for change to generate the needed "shock" for the process to take hold. Without providing a rationale about why things should be different and how the institution could be enhanced, leaders realized that change would be an uphill battle. These activities provided opportunities for leaders to articulate the various challenges the institution faced and to present a rationale for action. Leaders at the transforming institutions understood that key groups on campus must recognize the need for action before they willingly participate. They knew that change for the sake of change is suspect in higher education.

Simply suggesting that the institution must change without providing a compelling reason for it did not generate a disconnect powerful enough to initiate sensemaking.

To make the case for change, leaders relied on a variety of strategies. At Sunshine, change leaders collected extensive data on student outcomes, postgraduation employment patterns, and student satisfaction. They compiled and presented these data at their various roundtables and retreats. Leaders at other institutions, on the other hand, relied on anecdotes and stories to make the case for change. The provost at one institution spent time talking to faculty across the campus to identify what he called the "common irritants" to which people in different units could relate. These stories helped people understand that the problems they were facing extended beyond a single unit and were of a greater magnitude than they originally thought. At Midwest, leaders used a combination of qualitative and quantitative information to make their case for change. Because of their financial situation, the racial incident, and enrollment trends, the shocks were readily recognizable to the campus. Without making a clear case for change, institutions may not create the shocks necessary to getting people to think differently.

CONCLUSION

Effecting transformational change is as much about new ideas and beliefs as it is about actions. The important task of getting people to adopt new mind-sets is a cognitive and intellectual process spurred by a set of activities that can be intentionally designed. Implementing transformation is not simply dependent upon university decision makers changing structures, policies, and reward systems. Merit pay alone does not induce new sense. An essential role for institutional change leaders is to intentionally design strategies that help people think differently and leave behind old ideas, assumptions, and mental models.

The experiences of the three institutions discussed here also suggest that outsiders play important roles in facilitating new thinking. Institutional leaders should not adopt a "go-it-alone" or hibernation attitude. External intervention can be productive if the outsiders are selected intentionally for their messages and viewpoints, and if leaders design ways to actively engage the differing perspectives.

In addition, the insights from this chapter suggest that more people, not fewer, need to be engaged to effect transformation, reinforcing the ideas of collaborative leadership, discussed in the next chapter. Keeping the responsibility for leading change to a few high-level administrators does not create the widespread opportunities for participation and interaction needed for collective, institution-wide sensemaking. Revealing a final product or a well-crafted plan produced by a few does little to encourage sensemaking and does not allow for a large number of individuals to go through the processes to develop new understandings.

CHAPTER 4

Five Core Strategies
for Transformation

This chapter focuses on the core strategies essential for transformation. They are the intentional mechanisms, processes, and tools available to campus leaders to effect major change that is deep, pervasive, and cultural and that occurs over time. As we have noted, our thesis is that transformational change is different from other types of change. Although research on other types of change can be helpful, it only tells part of the story of transformation. This chapter explores the five core strategies that surfaced across the transforming institutions and that played fundamental roles in launching and sustaining transformation efforts.

To set the context for these strategies, we first briefly review the change literature. Then we present five core strategies—senior administrative support, collaborative leadership, flexible vision, visible action, and staff development—and provide rich illustrations of them across the six transforming institutions in the ACE project.

WHAT RESEARCHERS SAY ABOUT
INTENTIONAL CHANGE

A summary of the research on intentional change suggests seven strategies as important (although various writers identify many more with less agreement): (1) a willing president or strong administrative leadership, (2) a collaborative process, (3) persuasive and effective communication, (4) a motivating vision, (5) long-term orientation, (6) rewards, and (7) essential support structures (see, for example, Cowan, 1993; Kaiser & Kaiser, 1994; Roberts, Wergin, & Adam, 1993; Taylor & Koch, 1996). There is no agreement in the literature about which of the strategies are the most effective or how they might work together. We used these various strategies as a starting point to understand better the keys to transformation. Some of these strategies emerged as important within the transformational change process, such as strong administrator leadership, whereas others were modified, such as a motivating vision and mission. Still others seemed less important, such as incentives and rewards.

Strong administrative leadership (often cited as presidential leadership) refers to active participation by those with authority over budgets, personnel, and institutional priorities. It is well acknowledged in the literature on change that having support of the president and other individuals with positional power allows the change process to occur more quickly because these people can secure human and financial resources and focus institutional priorities (Cowan, 1993; Fisher, Tack, & Wheeler, 1988; Kerr & Gade, 1986; Lindquist, 1978; Lovett, 1993). Although grassroots change can occur, especially on campuses with strong faculty or student groups, these change efforts can be met with resistance if there is not buy-in from those with positional power (Kerr, 1984). Even though colleges and universities have been described as organized anarchies (Cohen & March, 1986) in which change can happen haphazardly (or often not at all), several studies have illustrated that change can be facilitated through the support of individuals in positions of power (Birnbaum, 1992; Kerr, 1984).

However, thinking about the role of leadership as it relates to change is expanding, moving beyond simply a strong and willing president or strong administrative leadership. Leadership is viewed as a *collaborative process* (Bensimon & Neumann, 1993; Cowan, 1993; Curry, 1992; Lindquist, 1978). Collaboration typically refers to involving stakeholders throughout the organization in both designing and implementing the key activities in the change process. Higher education has long had a collaborative decision-making structure, in particular through its shared governance structures. However, the extent of collaboration varies as it relates to change. For example, collaboration sometimes entails vision setting; other times, collaboration means delegating work with no real authority over direction, goals, or process. Although not clearly defined and inconsistent across institutions (Birnbaum, 1988; Eckel, 1998), when done right, collaborative leadership appears to be significant. Studies within the corporate environment have illustrated the importance of collaborative processes for commitment, empowerment, and engagement of individuals with thorough knowledge of the organization, as well as for the development of momentum (Gardenswartz & Rowe, 1994).

Persuasive and effective communication refers to the activity in which the change process is described and made understandable to constituents (Lindquist, 1978). An effective campus leader might write articles for newsletters, give speeches, hold town meetings, and send notes via e-mail. Developing a communication strategy fosters an understanding of change necessary for action. The benefits of communication include fostering buy-in to facilitating collaborative leadership to developing relationships (Curry, 1992).

Probably the most commonly described process within change is *a motivating vision*. It is also highly linked to other organizational activities such as planning, institutional communication, leadership, reward structures, and hiring processes. Vision is mentioned as central to accomplishing these activities (Kaiser & Kaiser, 1994; Kerr, 1984; St. John, 1991). Because change often invites risk and an uncertain future or destination, having a compelling reason for change and a proposed direction is crucial. A motivating vision or mission can become the blueprint and compass for many employees. This compass allows people to move toward something new and beneficial, not just unknown.

Another factor evident from the literature is that change is not likely to happen quickly; it takes time. Several problems related to not having *a long-term orientation* have been connected to the failure of many change efforts, such as (1) providing incentives only for the short-term effort, (2) not developing strategies to capture and hold attention through distractions, (3) disillusionment when not preparing people for the long-term commitment, and (4) turnover in leadership before the change effort takes root (Lindquist, 1978; Millar & Roberts, 1993). The literature repeatedly reviews how institutions fail at change because they do not engage the process with a long-term perspective (Ramaley, 1995).

Rewards or *incentives* are described in the literature as key ways to encourage employees to channel efforts from existing activities to new or additional activities. The incentives can range from computer upgrades, summer salaries, and merit increases to conference travel money and public recognition and awards (Roberts, Wergin, & Adam, 1993; Tierney & Rhoads, 1993). The rationale is that although a motivating vision or mission provides people with a compelling reason to engage the change process, incentives can provide vehicles for continuing or enabling change. For example, enabling people to attend a conference on assessment might be the necessary incentive to have them be able to facilitate change (McMahon & Caret, 1997).

Developing *support structures*, such as creating new centers or positions, realigning roles, and reallocating resources, is central for sustaining and achieving change (Curry, 1992; Guskin, 1994; St. John, 1991). Developing these support structures allows for the focus, effort, and resources needed to be committed (McMahon & Caret, 1997).

WHAT WE FOUND: CORE STRATEGIES OF TRANSFORMATION

Taking the literature as a starting point, we identified five core strategies common to transforming institutions: (1) senior administrative support, (2) collaborative leadership, (3) flexible vision, (4) staff development, and (5) visible action. Together they make up the essential elements of transformation. If the institutions studied did not develop any one of these capacities, their transformation efforts suffered.

We also discovered an underlying connection between these five strategies; they are all approaches to making people think differently. For example, staff development exposes people to new concepts. Collaborative leadership, through the constant interaction and involvement of large numbers of people, also facilitates sensemaking. Having a flexible vision allows people on campus to challenge their thinking and to test assumptions, which also results in new ways of thinking. Throughout this chapter we highlight the ways in which the five core strategies are essential to helping people think differently.

Supportive senior administration focuses on the actions that individuals in top leadership positions contribute to transformation. Among the key elements were focusing attention on related issues, providing resources, guiding the process, and creating new administrative structures to support the efforts. *Collaborative leadership* refers to individuals beyond those holding formal leadership positions who are involved in the change initiative from conception to implementation. With *flexible vision*, leaders develop a flexible yet clear and desirable picture of the future that includes goals and objectives related to that future's implementation. An essential key to flexible vision is creating a picture of the future that is clear and succinct but that does not foreclose possible opportunities that might emerge. Our idea originally focused solely on the broader topic of vision but was expanded as we learned that visions must not be overly firm and must evolve as transformation progresses. *Staff development* refers to programmatic efforts for individuals to learn certain skills or gain new knowledge related to the change agenda. Finally, *visible action* refers to progress in the change process that marks continual advancement toward the articulated goals of the transformation agenda. Activities must be visible and widely promoted so that individuals can see that the change remains an important institutional undertaking over time and that progress is continuing. Visible action is an important strategy for building momentum and keeping the institution focused on the tasks at hand. A more detailed description of the characteristics of these five strategies better defines these strategies and provides a more clear understanding prior to illustrating their use.

Senior administrative support appears to play the same role in transformational change as in other types of change; leaders provide necessary resources and shape institutional priorities. Not surprisingly, senior administrative support may be more important to transformation than to lesser types of change. For example, the literature on incremental change acknowledged that changes could be facilitated through senior administrative support, yet many successful changes occur without it. In contrast, senior administrative support is a necessary strategy for the creation of transformational change. An effort that depends strongly on any one or few individuals is vulnerable to turnover or diverted attention. As we found, this potential can make transformational change precarious because presidents and vice presidents frequently leave in the midst of change. As the efforts of project institutions demonstrated, transformational change takes more than five years to occur; the likelihood of a president or other senior administrators leaving during this time period is quite high. This represents a challenge for transformational change efforts. As presidents leave, they need to be aware that their efforts at change are likely to collapse unless they work closely with the incoming president. Boards need to think more carefully about transition plans when they are responsible for institutions that are undertaking transformational-level change. Perhaps one of the most important approaches is making the board responsible for the continuity needed by key administrators.

The use of collaborative leadership as a strategy to create transformational change operated differently from descriptions of collaborative processes predominant in the change literature. First, collaboration regarding transformation extends beyond asking for advice. With transformational change, collaboration entails empowerment—more than advisory, but real decision-making authority. Unless individuals are deeply involved in the formation, decisions, approval, and implementation, there is little hope that the campus will be transformed. Buy-in, crucial for most types of change, is facilitated in transformation through a highly participatory

collaborative leadership process. Campuses should aim for an empowerment approach whereby decision making is truly shared. Collaborative
leadership also helps people think differently. By involving more people
in the process of change, new mental models are extended onto greater
numbers of individuals.

Flexible vision is a particular type of vision that provides a clear direction for the institution yet is adaptable and opportunistic and does not
foreclose opportunities that might advance the institution. What we
found, however, is that based on the highly collaborative leadership process necessary for transformation, visions were not determined by a single
leader or a group of leaders at the top; nor were they presented in final
form. Instead, a process evolved whereby leaders set a direction (typically
through asking targeted questions) that was flexible and opportunistic and
open to the "right kind" of modification. However, which modifications
were constructive and which were destructive varied across institutions
and even within institutions over the life span of the transformation
efforts. As new people gained new understandings and created different
meanings related to the change and the institution moved forward,
emerging perspectives and opportunities added to the emergent flexible
vision. Flexible vision is an alternative to a more defined vision precisely
because of dual characteristics of openness and direction. However, there
is a paradox in the notion of the flexible vision. Within a transformational
change process, one would think that a highly defined vision would be
critical because a very unstable or new future is being created and common sense would dictate that a well-defined vision is needed to move
forward. Campuses that define a clear, tight vision often feel that they
have made more progress initially (and often, they do make a faster start
toward transformation) than those that have a flexible vision. Many campuses expressed concern that they spent too much time at the beginning
without a clear roadmap, having discussions about what changes mean
but making no progress or not knowing where they are going. This initial
flexibility turns out to be important because it provides space and time
for people to think differently. It also helps the institution become more
constructively opportunistic, which helps to advance the transformation
agenda. Patience is critical within the process, especially in the beginning
when a lack of any clear vision prevails.

Staff development is a strategy for organizational change not discussed
as often within the incremental literature. However, it was one of the key
five strategies for creating transformational change within the project
institutions. Learning is critical within a transformational change process.
As other types of lesser changes occur, most people can make adjustments

without needing different skills or new knowledge; thus these changes do not require as much intentional development. On campuses that were transforming, staff development was a centerpiece of campus efforts. Staff development differed across institutions in its intensity and depth, the extent to which it was voluntary, and the number of people that were involved.

Taking visible action was a strategy unique to transformational change, not appearing in reviews of other processes. Much of this process is related to the long-term orientation of transformation. Because of the slower nature of transformational change, campuses can lose enthusiasm and motivation in the absence of readily identifiable markers of progress. With other types of change, usually some evidence of change is visible quickly. However, in transformation, because of the magnitude of the change agenda, the need to develop a flexible vision, and the difficulty of the tasks ahead, a campus can easily believe that it is making little progress. Therefore, campuses that were successful had leaders who set achievable interim goals and found ways to evidence progress. They then proceeded to communicate this progress widely across campus.

The next section puts these ideas into practice by illustrating the diversity in which these strategies were enacted. We describe each campus's experience, starting with Middle State University, followed by Metropolitan University, Midwest College, Archdiocese University, Civic State University, and Sunshine Community College. Metropolitan and Sunshine are described in less detail in some sections because these two institutions are used as case examples to illustrate the Mobile Model in chapter 7.

SENIOR ADMINISTRATIVE SUPPORT

Senior administrative support made several essential contributions to the transformation process. Senior campus administrators provided necessary financial resources and created incentives; they focused institutional attention and set priorities; they invited collaboration and facilitated collaborative leadership; they framed the institutional change initiative in meaningful ways that did not place blame; and they provided a consistent message about the ways in which the proposed change would improve the institution. The experiences from the institutions illustrate the important roles that senior administrators played as stewards of change.

Middle State University

At Middle State University, senior administrators played key roles in gathering resources to support the transformation efforts. For example, they read what the legislature was interested in funding and secured from it resources earmarked for technology to support campus efforts. Without this ongoing search for external support, the change might not have been possible. As one person reported: "The university obtained state funds for an investment in technology nearly 10 years ago and has continued to seek supporting funds. Significant investment in desktop computers for faculty and computer labs for students has brought major change to the teaching-learning environment. Through the initial funding and subsequent investment, Middle State has become one of the leading universities in teaching with technology."

Senior administrators made available both money and human resources. Middle State's president created a new position for information technology that carries senior administrative responsibility for the development and support of all technology uses. Although financial and human supports were major components, philosophical support was also critical. The president and provost participated in ongoing faculty-led discussions about the principles appearing in *Scholarship Reconsidered* (Boyer, 1990). They engaged deans and department chairs in discussions about evaluating teaching, the role of different types of scholarship, and the reward system as they relate to becoming a premier teaching institution using technology. Symbolic support included recurring public commitments to the transformation agenda for the long haul. One faculty member commented that "this [commitment] made us see that his agenda was not a flash in the pan. We had time to buy in over time and came to realize that the agenda was not going to change on a yearly basis."

Metropolitan University

At Metropolitan University, senior administrators were responsible for launching the initiative and facilitating the first conversations that began the process to identify common educational goals that would transcend departments and colleges. They provided important attention as the campus faced many important issues and, some would argue, faced a crisis: Should the institution focus on the 30 percent decline in enrollment that had occurred over the past two years, the troubling accreditation review, a perceived drop in research quality, town-gown problems, the mission's lack of clarity, poorly operating decision-making processes, the lack of interest and commitment to student learning, low campus morale, ingrained resistance to change created by previous administrations, or incoherence in the curriculum? In the words of one member of the campus community: "The President, Provost, and Board provided focus. There appeared to be an overwhelming number of problems and there needed to be someone to help us develop common ground about what we should focus our efforts on first and why. Everyone wanted to preserve the campus entrepreneurial spirit, but also make changes in a focused manner rather than simply reacting to various circumstances."

Similar to Middle State, the senior administrators at Metropolitan secured outside funds at a time when the institution could not internally reallocate existing monies. They received a $250,000 grant from the Fund for the Improvement of Postsecondary Education, a $200,000 grant for institution-wide reform from the National Science Foundation and $150,000 from a corporate foundation. Senior administrators continually sought funds to support the transformation efforts. In addition to providing needed resources, the recognition by outside funders added important legitimacy to campus efforts. Administrators used these grants to leverage publicity in the national and local media, which added to the momentum.

Finally, leaders at Metropolitan played important roles in shaping the change process. The provost and the associate vice provost took the pulse of the campus and planned activities and events that encouraged the colleges and departments to take a serious look at their curricula and make necessary changes. They also obtained the support and participation of key decision-making bodies on campus and shepherded the process through key campus constituents.

Midwest College

Midwest College's senior administration established institutional priorities by calling attention to the state of the college. Many campus members noted that no one else, on or off campus, was going to push the institution to establish new institutional priorities. Senior administrators played this critical role. Once the president had framed the challenge, he charged the campus community with creating the solutions. According to one member of the campus, "he planted the seed and then stepped back and let it take root." At Midwest, senior administrators, particularly the president and the dean (the college's chief academic administrator), invited people to shape the transformation, and thus the institution's agenda, and eventually established the high expectation for involvement and leadership from the faculty *and* staff. Thus, senior administrators were crucial in fostering the collaborative leadership that emerged. Midwest's senior administrators also obtained major grants from the Teagle Foundation,

The Upton Foundation, the W. K. Kellogg Foundation, The Alden Trust, The William Randolf Hearst Foundation, and the state's Department of Education, helping to support the effort and give it external validation.

Archdiocese University

Archdiocese University followed a more traditional model of senior administrative support. For example, the planning process began with the executive cabinet—the president, provost, vice president for student affairs, vice president for business affairs, and vice president for planning. This group scanned the environment and developed a set of campus priorities. As a longtime member of the campus, the president had a well-informed notion about changes for the campus, realizing that quality, reputation, and sharpening the institutional identity were critical. When these priorities were disseminated to the campus, there was less freedom to alter the change initiative. Instead, the individual divisions were asked to develop objectives and programs to implement the strategic goals, an approach that adhered to the norms of the Catholic institution. This method illustrates that, depending on the circumstances and the campus culture, senior administration may effectively play a more traditional, hierarchical role within a climate of shared governance. More on this variation appears in chapter 6.

The president of Archdiocese considered fostering collaboration among the members of the community as a key role of senior administration. He invited people to participate in the change initiative by personally sending a memo to every member of the campus community. The senior leadership modeled collaboration by having the provost, president, and vice president for student affairs work together closely to provide key leadership, something that had not happened in the past. All three continually reiterated their unified support for the changes at meetings, public events, and ceremonies and jointly, visibly shaped the process.

Senior administrators at Archdiocese also obtained external support for the transformation process, mostly from local foundations and state agencies. They also made new resources available by spending $5 million of their quasi-endowment to support the transformation efforts. Not only was the senior administration key to external resources, but in freeing internal resources, as one person noted, "The Board made available additional resources because the president made convincing arguments about our ability to move forward with the change initiative. Given the limited budgets of the divisions, the special resources advanced by the Board become critical, really a turning point for gaining momentum for the change initiative."

Most people at Archdiocese agreed that institutionalization would have been difficult, if not impossible, without senior administrative support; financial support, board buy-in, rewards, and setting institutional priorities were critical elements for beginning and sustaining change, according to the project team at Archdiocese University. As one person commented, "The support from the very top puts the change initiative on everybody's agenda whether they want it to be there or not. That is how things had to get started."

Civic State University

For Civic State, senior administrative support involved priority setting, providing a consistent message, framing the change initiative for others, obtaining funds, and inviting participation. Similar to Metropolitan, Civic State had a plethora of issues ranging from lack of community support and declining quality of instruction to disheartened faculty and an out-of-date infrastructure, among other issues. The senior leaders helped to create connections between some of these issues, reducing the number of items needing to be addressed to two central issues. From there, the senior administrators made speeches and wrote white papers outlining their support for the change process, trying to assure the community that they should take the risk and join the movement to change. In addition, this process of constantly discussing and writing about change helped to frame the process in multiple ways, which brought more people to the movement as the unique ways the initiative was framed resonated with new individuals. Senior leaders kept saying the same message in different ways to reach more people. One person commented on the success of the constant messages sent by senior administrators: "By framing the institutional initiative for people on campus repeatedly, people understood where they were headed and felt more confident and secure. Faculty are able to see connections between the changes underway and institutional enhancement."

The funds provided through four major grants secured by senior administrators provided not only money but also important recognition and pride to a campus that was unaccustomed to national attention, which in turn created energy for the change process. Following the example of inviting participation, Civic State's provost and president asked faculty to design a teaching and learning center that would support curricular and technological changes. This direct invitation and encouragement in a specific area helped open the door to participation across the change initiative.

Sunshine Community College

At Sunshine, senior administrative support included designing the change process, garnering financial resources, creating incentives and rewards, framing the change message, creating new structures to support the effort, securing resources, and articulating a philosophy that values what the campus currently does well, which in turn made people feel appreciated. Throughout the process, senior leaders scanned the environment to determine if new grants could be obtained to support new ideas that emerged in the planning process. Senior administrators saw their role as enabling the development of good ideas with resources. Another way for enabling change was through the alteration of rewards and the creation of incentives. Senior administrators used external grant money to establish incentives to become more learning centered. In addition to internal grant processes, there were also opportunities to attend conferences, earn summer salaries, and the like. The president constantly articulated the importance of the change initiative and took a lead role in writing to all the members of the college community about the change project. In addition, the president provided resources for one key recommendation from the roundtables—to create a new position, vice president for institutional transformation, to provide resources and focus for the change initiative. Finally, campus leaders realized early in the process the importance of validation. Individuals commented on how only senior leaders could have obtained the financial support for a new office. Many faculty and administrators believed they were already doing well, and by recognizing this fact, senior leaders made people feel worthwhile during the change process.

COLLABORATIVE LEADERSHIP

Collaborative leadership may have been the most complex strategy for institutions to initiate and sustain. First, collaborative leadership played itself out differently depending if institutions adopted a bottom-up or top-down strategy. Among the six institutions represented in this study, four took a top-down approach (strong administrative presence) and two used a bottom-up approach (low administrative presence). Both can be successful, but determining which will work best shapes the process and depends on individual institutional culture and context. Second, transformation occurs when leaders at multiple levels work compatibly. On each campus, leaders engaged simultaneously on cross-campus teams, task forces, and committees, while also encouraging departmental and individual faculty leadership. Larger campuses simply required more leaders because of their complexity.

A set of conditions needs to be in place for collaborative leadership to flourish, the most important one being trust. Without trust between faculty and administrators, between various faculty groups, and between staff, faculty, and administrators, few transformation efforts would have succeeded. The intensity and focus of collaborative leadership efforts varied and was fluid. It occurred both throughout the transformation process and episodically around important issues and at key points in time. An important aspect of collaborative leadership was encouraging and reconciling diverse opinions and creating opportunities to publicly criticize the transformation agenda and process. Being open to challenge, criticism, and different ways of operating also was critical for creating a collaborative leadership environment. Developing a common language and shared goals helped facilitate communication and mutual understanding, which is important for collaborative leadership. Teams or task forces that are established need to be representative of the campus constituents. Efforts at collaboration were set back if the leadership make-up was missing any key groups or if the proportion of certain groups did not match the campus. However, the specifics of who should participate and in what ways varied because of campus culture (see chapter 6 for further discussion).

Middle State University

Middle State is a perfect example of a process that was truly grass roots and in which there was little top-down control. Collaborative leadership was developed through campuswide roundtables and dialogues, departmental leadership, and individual faculty leaders. These three different levels of leadership made the process collaborative and helped spread responsibility for setting direction and realizing change throughout the institution. The campus began building a collaborative environment through roundtables and cross-campus dialogues. One of its main efforts was a series of mini-roundtables with a wide range of campus constituents invited to talk about institutional goals and determine direction. In other efforts, different groups of people worked together, such as faculty from a range of departments who drafted *A New Day*, a document that outlined new definitions of scholarship and faculty roles as related to teaching and technology and which served as a mandate for change. This document emerged from the faculty themselves rather than being implemented from the top.

However, this collaborative process of meeting for roundtable dialogues and for committee meetings was not without its toll, as one member of the campus explained: "Change in higher education is a long, difficult process. One of our team members pointed out that democracy is slow. We have also learned that change is not likely to take place from unilateral approaches nor is it likely to take place in any consistent manner. We have developed strategies that allow groups to emerge and move at a pace that is appropriate for them."

Campus change leaders encouraged departments and faculty to take leadership responsibility. Initial funds were invested in departments, in decentralized workshops, in technology that faculty selected, and in an infrastructure that supported a diverse area of technology initiatives based on individual faculty interest. Leaders encouraged and supported individuals and groups of faculty who showed interest in advancing a campuswide technology agenda. At no time was anyone mandated by the administration to do anything. Their approach was to encourage innovation as it grew from faculty ranks. Different initiatives sprang up within different disciplines to respond to different needs. One faculty member commented that "the initial investment in the departments allowed the technology decisions to best match the needs of the faculty, the students and the discipline." Twenty of the forty-seven departments voluntarily altered rewards structures to follow *Scholarship Reconsidered* (Boyer, 1990). There was no specific directive from senior administration. Instead, university promotion and tenure committees, led by faculty, rallied support for the change. As one person noted, the redesign of History 150 reflected the widespread leadership typical throughout the process:

History 150 is a one-semester course required of all students in our General Studies Program. It is often taught in large sections. Faculty in the history department decided to completely redesign the course using technology. This is a success story because in the early stages of our technology efforts, the humanities were not as strongly involved as professional departments. Now we see a strong move to redesign courses in History, English, Modern Languages, and Psychology.

Collaborative leadership at Middle State extended beyond departments to individual faculty, as this example illustrates:

The role of visionary faculty members was key in shaping our change process. In the school of nursing, for instance, the entire curriculum has been reshaped around technology. All faculty cite [one faculty member] as the reason they made such changes. She started by creating videos and continued to design new software and finally a totally new web based curriculum. Her leadership, her vision and her determination brought about a new way of thinking in her department and made them leaders in the nation for technology based nursing curriculum. There are many similar stories of faculty members who took advantage of the opportunities that technology presented and institutional support; these are the core efforts that led to significant strides in incorporating technology into teaching and learning.

Metropolitan University

At Middle State, the informal environment and easy interaction among faculty and administrators made collaborative leadership natural, whereas at Metropolitan University, leaders needed to construct and foster collaboration more because of its autonomous culture. At Metropolitan, shared goals and the open exchange of information were noted as the foundations of building trust. Faculty and administrators believed trust to be extremely important to institution-wide change, particularly at an institution with such a tradition of autonomy. One person commented about the importance of trust for developing collaborative leadership: "The independence of the various schools and units presents a challenge for developing the trust needed for interdisciplinary efforts."

The transformation process began with a large institution-wide committee of faculty, administrators, and students; however, the entire community was kept informed, and their feedback was invited from the beginning.

Central administrators encouraged collaborative leadership by asking each unit to design its own curricular changes around agreed-upon goals that were identified by the initial task force. In addition, rather than dictate a centrally coordinated implementation formula, senior administrators encouraged each college to develop its own review process to identify the extent to which it already met the institution's Common Academic Charter objectives, develop its own implementation process, and create its own system of assessment. One administrator noted: "We strongly believed that our community needed to identify its own educational goals. With the project's potential to transform undergraduate education, community support for the basic foundation was essential, particularly given the lack of common ground." Campus leaders realized that not all units would take responsibility for implementing the proposed changes equally. One administrator commented:

The change process has occurred slowly and unevenly. Some of that was deliberate—so the campus could achieve buy in by slowly widening the group of faculty and administrators involved. We realized that true buy in and to actually achieve the goal of transforming the undergraduate education would take time. To rush ahead would result in window dressing rather than substantive curricular change. Some units more easily see the connection of the changes to their goals and forge ahead. Other units hope the whole initiative will go away and they chose to play a waiting game. In the end, units will own this change; it will not be foisted upon them. But, this does lead to some tension about balancing top-down pressure and bottom up enthusiasm. There is a temptation to use top down pressure on units that are waiting.

Metropolitan's cross-departmental interest groups are another example of collaborative leadership. These groups allowed interested faculty to share similar concerns and engage in collective problem solving. Change leaders at Metropolitan made sure to support such efforts with resources. Interest group leaders received a stipend, and workshops sponsored by the interest groups were guaranteed a small budget.

Metropolitan did achieve a balance between administrator and faculty-driven efforts. Similar to Middle State, individual faculty leadership was central to Metropolitan's success. Faculty within each unit were willing to talk to each other about the curriculum and to work toward shared unit goals and expectations.

Midwest College

At Midwest College, collaborative leadership was established from the beginning, with the president setting up criteria for the campus to chart its course and the faculty taking responsibility immediately to develop the change initiative. At this small campus, the initiative had to be approved by the whole faculty. No small committee or group was responsible for the effort; it was a campuswide approach. The entire faculty ratified the set of learning outcomes, as well as an implementation plan.

The collaborative leadership at Midwest College continued through the work of various task forces composed of faculty, staff, and students. The project work was kicked off by a day for developing a "College Compact." Everyone in the entire campus community was invited, and almost all faculty, staff, and students attended. Anyone who was interested was asked to be part of the ongoing deliberations, which meant receiving drafts of documents and being asked to discuss issues that emerged. The student senate, staff senate, and entire faculty eventually endorsed the compact.

Archdiocese University

At Archdiocese University, an array of factors contributed to collaborative leadership, including presidential invitation, focus groups, retreats and conferences, working groups, the development of a planning and policy committee, and cross-functional teams. Archdiocese's senior administrators saw fostering collaboration among community members as one of their main responsibilities. The president worked with senior administrators to put together teams to lead their efforts and to develop strategies to engage more people across the campus in the change process. The campus community then participated in focus groups to provide feedback on the initial plan. One faculty member reflected on the strength of the initial one-day conference for helping to develop collaborative leadership and on the importance of leadership throughout the campus:

Faculty shared ideas, identified problems and reflected on what kind of knowledge, insights, and attitudes towards learning students should acquire during this initial phase of their education. Major decisions were also made such as altering the number of students in first year writing courses from 25 to 15. A faculty member in English made a strong case for the change [that] really illustrated leadership. Faculty around campus realized the importance of students developing strong writing skills in the first year. Although this would require a large redistribution of funds to the English department, faculty across campus realized this was the right decision. This would not have happened if we had not all been working together, collaboratively.

Beyond the initial retreat and subsequent focus groups, faculty members and staff took ownership of the overall planning activity. The institution formed cross-functional project teams of faculty and staff to coordinate the curricular and cocurricular initiatives to transform the first-year experience. Two of the six faculty members on the project team chaired educational policy committees of the faculty senate and the College of Arts and Sciences. Their role was to work with the appropriate faculty committees to secure faculty support for changes in curriculum and academic policies. These various faculty leaders—on teams and heading committees—created a network of well-placed collaborating leaders throughout the campus. Staff from various student affairs units took institutional responsibility, something they had traditionally left to the faculty. A senior administrator described the value of collaboration:

The interesting thing about the task force is that some of the best academic ideas came from student affairs and some of the most interesting student affairs ideas came from faculty. These conversations would never have happened unless we set out to be collaborative and cross functional with our planning teams. We wound up with a whole new series of ideas, never generated on this campus before. People were impressed and convinced the process works.

Civic State University

Civic State had a broad-based discussion and collaborative agenda throughout its transformation process, facilitated by a multilayered approach to collaboration. Campus leaders initially appointed a team of nineteen individuals, representing groups across campus, to lead one part of the initiative. From the beginning, a broad group of faculty, staff, and students expressed interest in shaping the future direction by attending roundtable discussions and a symposium about the change initiative. Senior administrators encouraged people they knew were skeptical about the project to attend the roundtables, sending a clear message to the campus that all voices were welcome. As a staff member recounted: "The project team wanted faculty and staff across the campus to inform the future actions. This was accomplished through the symposium where participation was broadened, wider campus input of the change initiative was received and recommendations for accommodating changes encouraged." In the weeks that followed the symposium, draft documents were sent around campus for refinement and debate. Only after many rounds of input from all members of the community was the final draft sent to the faculty senate, staff senate, and entire faculty for endorsement. Many faculty were asked to volunteer for later-forming ad hoc committees and working groups. Because faculty were empowered by administrators to make decisions and provided the room to do so, many people volunteered.

Several later focused strategies were also initiated. For example, at the start of each academic year, the Center for Teaching Excellence sponsored events to bring people together, create a sense of community, and provide input on various aspects of the change initiative. The campus also began a series of reading groups as a way to facilitate faculty leadership. Small groups of faculty members read and discussed a topic related to the campus change effort. This process intellectually engaged faculty as leaders and was perhaps the most effective way the campus developed faculty leadership. The success of reading groups led to subsequent symposia and engaged an even larger set of people in the reading and discussion of ideas related to their change efforts.

Sunshine Community College

Sunshine Community College developed a collaborative process through the use of a cross-college leadership team, campuswide workshops, symposia, and roundtables. As on other campuses, Sunshine's president personally invited campus participants to attend each event. All plans and ideas were vetted through important campus groups, encouraging people to participate informally and influence the outcomes and process. An eleven-person leadership team was formed with members representing a range of campus groups, including the senate leadership and the four campuses of the college. The leadership team members facilitated a series of roundtables at which they described why change was necessary and asked for feedback. More than three hundred people attended. One campus member reflecting on the roundtable commented: "The energy generated from these voluntary interactions, in which we were equal partners with equally strong voices, was powerful and gratifying." A call for leadership for a group of four action teams was made, and 180 faculty and staff volunteered to continue to spearhead the effort and to supplement the work of the leadership team. Later, the institution formed four additional action teams, all led by faculty and midlevel staff. The college adopted the language of collaboration and worked to ensure that their efforts were open. Many people echoed the president's view on collaboration:

Collaboration will strengthen our results because it invites differing opinions to the discussion processes and gives more faculty, staff and administrators a chance to craft and own the change process. Leaders must be committed to the collaborative process if they are to change the agenda itself. They must build trust with their colleagues as professionals and to rely on their judgment. This builds unity and when it is time to implement specific changes, trust will expedite, rather than inhibit implementation.

One key aspect to ensuring collaborative leadership was common to all transforming institutions but was epitomized at Sunshine—the importance of developing a shared language and vocabulary. Many people commented that a shared language reduced anxiety because people understood what was expected and improved communication. They noted that previous change initiatives had failed at Sunshine because there was not a way for people to communicate clearly about the proposed change.

FLEXIBLE VISION

Flexible vision—a vision that is consistent and has a targeted direction, and yet is opportunistic and does not foreclose important opportunities—

can seem counterintuitive to the belief that good leadership sets a vision and charts a decisive course. Yet creating a flexible vision that allows details and variations to emerge is the essential pattern, not a detailed vision of the future. In this project, half of the transforming institutions began their efforts with a small leadership group, often senior administrators, who develop an initial plan on which they obtained feedback. The other half initiated their efforts with large cross-campus planning that involved all major constituencies in the initial design. The process was not based on the size of the campus.

An important component of the flexible vision process is developing multiple venues for campus feedback. Providing opportunities to influence the direction of the process helped ensure the direction's robustness and allowed it to take advantage of opportunities unforeseen by campus change leaders. Each transforming campus developed such multiple mechanisms, including periodic retreats, surveys, roundtable conversations, and informal processes of asking team members to talk with their colleagues. Change leaders also developed strategies to communicate and disseminate the flexible vision to the campus, which proved challenging, as reaching a majority of individuals who pay different amounts of attention at any one time is difficult at best. However, each institution was able to devise a successful communications approach, often through trial and error.

Some institutions had an easy time moving beyond having a traditional vision to creating a flexible one. For example, at institutions that were smaller or more informal and tended to operate without documents or written vision statements, campus direction was emergent and opportunistic.

Middle State University

The leaders of Middle State chose not to develop a clear, detailed statement of the future. Instead they set a broad course—ensuring computer competency for all students—and provided the resources to departments and individual faculty to determine their own best ways to move forward. The leaders were steadfast in their long-term commitment and made that fact widely know. Their change strategies reflected this laissez-faire approach. Although they established a campus committee to initially design the change process and oversee it, obtaining feedback and setting up campus roundtables, for example, they realized that a single committee would be not effective in promoting the flexible vision. Instead, each individual, in his or her own role—as dean, department chair, faculty senator, or committee member—worked to keep the issue public and to bring focus to the issue. The leaders knew the campus would not respond to central edicts.

Metropolitan University

At Metropolitan, the centerpiece of its flexible vision was an agreed-upon set of general education outcomes. Once leaders had consensus on these goals, they designed a flexible process that allowed each autonomous college to move forward in its own way. Campus leaders set the parameters for action but left the specifics up to each college. The leaders started with three pilot programs, gave them credit and recognition, and rewarded their work. Later, through the use of campus cross-department interest groups, the change leaders were able to cross-fertilize thinking and action, helping good ideas spread throughout the institution. This design allowed members of the community to connect various issues while still working autonomously and to tap into a widely shared belief about common educational objectives. Their flexible vision was crafted in such a way that the adoption of and progress on the educational goals would have been acceptable in many different ways. The autonomous colleges did not have to abide by a common, rigid plan, and they knew they could design unique responses to fit their own operating styles. Campus leaders created a newsletter especially for the transformation agenda to disseminate good ideas, promote and reinforce the common key elements, and encourage continued experimentation. This vehicle ensured access to the information by the various autonomous schools.

Midwest College

Midwest College's president did not develop a vision for the institution. Instead, he developed six criteria to guide the campus in its work: work toward consensus among the faculty; consistency with the best of long-standing values of the college and emerging educational needs in society; responsiveness to issues of social justice and diversity; adherence to principles of good practice in undergraduate education; a cost-effective delivery system; and the clear promise of generating enthusiasm among and support of students, alumni, and other potential supporters of the college. The criteria resulted in a template that evolved as the work progressed and new challenges surfaced. Working within these criteria, the faculty developed a new academic vision statement for the college and adopted it by majority vote of 78 percent. At Midwest, part of the process to keep the plan flexible and to be opportunistic was to obtain feedback from national organizations and outside expert consultants. One member of the community commented that "we actively seek external consultation and advice for our vision and plans."

Archdiocese University

For Archdiocese, the flexible vision emerged in a way similar to Metropolitan University. Although the senior administrators set the outline for action and developed a set of guiding principles, the university went about advancing them through an inclusive process. To oversee the long-range plan, the university appointed a planning and policy committee, consisting of global, forward thinkers representing all areas of the institution. New people rotate on and off the committee from time to time to ensure fresh ideas. Leaders also encouraged different groups of faculty and staff to form task forces to work together. These various task forces worked toward adopting the objectives in their own areas, such as writing across the curriculum, the first three-semester experience, and various technology efforts. Archdiocese's plan changed over time to emphasize more strongly different elements such as developing the mobile computing center, academic quality, and interactive teaching—none of which were significant parts of the initial efforts.

Many people commented on the importance of the plan changing over time to meet unforeseen ideas. One noted:

We learned quickly that it would be difficult to accomplish what we wanted without an extensive, but flexible plan. The introduction of the mobile computing for all undergraduates, one of the most promising components of our change initiative, was not begun until we had completed a lengthy and expensive planning process. It involved preparing over several months, with the help of an outside consultant and a long-range technology plan. The plan then served as our guide in improving our technological infrastructure, reshaping from the bottom up the existing computing organization, training the faculty, securing funding for the project from the Board, and taking a host of other preparatory steps.

Part of keeping the planning open and opportunistic at Archdiocese included marking reports, minutes, and memos as drafts until there was ample opportunity for input across campus. The change leaders also made both their outcomes and their deliberations extremely accessible to everyone through the use of broadcast e-mail messages and the university's Web site. Archdiocese made a practice of having documents make several rounds before they became final.

Civic State University

Civic State began with a set of questions—about the role the university should play in the region, about the type of general education its students should receive, and about emerging trends in knowledge toward interdisciplinary discovery. By asking questions, and designing processes to find campuswide answers, leaders engaged people throughout the campus over time and developed more specific goals on which to advance that made up the building blocks of their transformation efforts. Leaders used various roundtables, seminars, and one-day meetings to elicit feedback and shape their directions. Unlike Metropolitan and Archdiocese, this campus's design for the future emerged out of these various conversations and information sessions. New items and initiatives were constantly developed and refined. One campus member commented that "the most important aspect of our plan is that it has been flexible and responsive. We have made changes along the way and capitalized on opportunities that we probably would not have if we had a traditional strategic plan and vision."

Sunshine Community College

At Sunshine, the flexible vision emerged out of a question posed to the campus about what it would mean for the community college to focus on learning and not teaching. To get to this question, the college for several previous years engaged in a range of dialogues about whom the campus should serve and the types of programs it should offer. It held numerous conversations on and off campus to address these questions. Sunshine's direction to become learning centered emerged early in the process. Leaders believed that by asking questions about improving student learning that challenged various sectors of the college to be introspective, the college would quickly embrace any progress. Rather than identifying components of a learning-centered community college and asking the campus to respond and accept or reject them, change leaders put that responsibility to the faculty and staff. What emerged out of that process reflected institutional beliefs and was explained in institutional language. Roundtables became a key mechanism for obtaining input on the college's direction. Hundreds of staff and faculty attended numerous events held over many years to explore ideas and test approaches. These conversations provided new insight into actions that would lead the college to become more learning centered. Notes from all roundtables and meeting were then compiled and circulated throughout the college, and all faculty and staff were invited to comment. New insights reflecting the conversations were incorporated into a document that was circulated college-wide. Based on the evolving documents, the leadership team developed a draft definition of a learning-centered community college. They decided to keep the statement as a perpetual draft to be revised as collective thinking evolved. Similar to Archdiocese University, Sunshine realized the power of marking documents as drafts for obtaining buy-in and support. However, this insight occurred by making initial mistakes. As one leadership team member noted: "Early on we sent around a report and no one said anything; we expected some people to comment. When we inquired about the lack of feedback, we were told that it was unclear that we wanted it since there was not draft on the document—the cover sheet got pulled off when distributed to lots of people. So, we learned, [put the word] 'draft' on everything."

These series of conversations eventually led to concrete action plans that could be implemented rapidly because they had already been vetted by the campus and reflected the good thinking and innovation of a wide range of faculty and staff. The leaders had taken the time needed to obtain input from all groups across campus, to achieve buy-in, to develop a common understanding of the change initiative, and to gain a common understanding of what being learning centered means for the college.

VISIBLE ACTION

The ways in which visible action played itself out varied tremendously across the six institutions because of different change agendas and the complexity of the institutions. In some instances, visible action involved celebrating the accomplishment of a specific goal; at other times, it meant creating a new office, obtaining a new grant, or creating a new position. Some campuses also created formal assessment processes as a way to demonstrate action; others used less-formal means. We learned that the specific content of the actions is not important; what matters is its timing. We saw important accomplishments demonstrated in the first year or two as a means to ensure the legitimacy and staying power of the change agenda. Campuses that were the most successful demonstrated action across several different areas; sometimes they did so concurrently, and other times sequentially. Leaders at transforming institutions promoted and publicized their accomplishments. Promoting successes was especially important on larger campuses, where the immediate impact may not be felt everywhere.

Middle State University

One of the most important visible changes at Middle State University was the purchase of computers for all faculty and the building of fifteen new electronic classrooms and several computer labs for students. Leaders worked hard to ensure that technology was visible everywhere on campus, making it hard not to acknowledge that a substantive change was well underway and that the institution had made significant investments not only in money but in people's time and the campus's infrastructure and space. Another visible action that Middle State undertook was the development of a faculty-led key document, *A New Day*, which described new approaches to faculty roles based on *Scholarship Reconsidered* (Boyer, 1990). It provided a visible product that people could begin to point to as an outcome of their discussions about change. One person commented on the power of that document as a visible product of transformational efforts. Other important visible changes included the incorporation of technology into a large percentage of departmental promotion and tenure guidelines.

Metropolitan University

Metropolitan used several mechanisms to make the advances visible. Faculty participated in discussion groups and attended campuswide forums, newsletters detailed the work of various groups, publicity about events was noted in on- and off-campus publications, and three colleges participated in pilot projects whose results were widely disseminated. The newsletter was a prominent way to communicate progress, especially within a large, decentralized campus such as Metropolitan. The pilot projects were key because the community saw talk turned into action. The implementation of the pilot projects was facilitated though detailed schedules publicly posted with set dates for when things had to occur. Each program was asked to develop and adhere to a schedule of implementation. Assessment of efforts was critical for ensuring and being able to describe action that had taken place. Every six months, units had to respond to requests for information related to their progress and achievements. Another key mechanism was on- and off-campus publicity. Every time a grant was received, this information was widely disseminated. Obtaining the grants in and of themselves marked important progress. Faculty members and administrators discussed the project at national conferences and placed articles in local and national papers. For a campus that had just gone through a humiliating poor accreditation, obtaining positive messages from external sources such as papers and conferences was important.

Midwest College

The faculty at Midwest College developed a document called the *College Plan* to solidify their various conversations and dialogues; it was adopted by a 90 percent vote of the faculty and overwhelmingly by the trustees. Both the document and the ensuing vote were important steps. The plan established a set of immediate changes that would lead to other visible changes. One change that people commented helped them realize that the change had occurred was the new academic calendar. Wednesdays are now reserved for activities that cannot be easily accommodated within regularly scheduled classes, such as service learning, portfolio assessment, and learning communities. The new calendar also includes a three-and-a-half-week intensive learning term as part of the second semester, during which students may enroll in only one course, allowing students and faculty to pursue special projects on or off campus free of conflicts with other course obligations.

Midwest followed a strategy similar to that of Metropolitan—assessing the change initiative in order to illustrate progress. Updates about campus progress were routinely sent to units. Another strategy capitalized on outside recognition, making efforts visible and prestigious. This approach was particularly successful at Midwest through the college-community responsibility scholarships to prospective students who participate in service programs. These scholarships were made possible by a partnership with an outside agency and helped make Midwest a leader in service learning. Having national visibility makes faculty and staff realize that important change has occurred. Recognition by outside groups was one of the most powerful approaches to creating visible action.

Archdiocese University

Archdiocese chose as one of its first goals to build on already-successful activities and programs directed toward first-year students. By building on a set of existing efforts and finding ways to make them synergetic, rather than creating something wholly new, they could generate visible results more quickly. The campus also established a Center for Academic Technology that developed and showcased ten curricular projects and seventeen academic departmental change initiatives, held a monthly seminar on technology and learning, and supported forty-three faculty fellows.

The center provided a focal point for technology-related efforts and had resources to publicize its project, programs, and initiatives. In addition to developing a highly visible first-year program and center immediately, the campus disseminated detailed and extensive summaries of deliberations of the project team over the campuswide information system to anyone willing to take an interest in the team's activities. One member of the project team commented on how the wide dissemination of the weekly notes from the meeting created a sense of progress on campus:

Many times people hear a committee is formed and think that nothing will come out of the committee or task force. In order to overcome this possible perception, we sent notes out each week detailing our deliberations to everyone on campus, to literally thousands of people. In addition, if a formal memo about the change initiative was sent out on campus, we forwarded it to everyone. If the president spoke about the initiative to external groups or on campus, we got a copy of the speech and forwarded to the email group. We sent quarterly reports to the regents and annual reports of the provost or vice president for student affairs to the same listserv. People knew that the project team was making progress and that we were connected and communicating with the senior administration and cross campus groups. There is nothing to generate commitment and motivation than people seeing actual progress being made.

Civic State University

Civic State was very successful at making progress visible. Previously, there had been discussion about changing the general education curriculum; debate went on for years, and few actual changes were made—at best tinkering, according to some on campus. Within two years, the university had added a three-term interdisciplinary course to the first-year experience, a capstone experience, and a community-based course in their junior year, all significant curricular changes. Faculty also developed "inquiry tracks" for the sophomore and junior years of the general education program as explicit linkages between the first-year and capstone courses. Like other campuses in the study, there had been many other proposed changes over the years, but for the initiative to be taken seriously, it had to show immediate progress.

Sunshine Community College

For Sunshine, failed earlier attempts at change made illustrating success all the more critical. One member of the campus commented on the need for visible change: "The leadership team became very aware of the need to balance talk and action. In all our planning, we have been careful to ensure that visible progress is being made on a number of fronts." The leadership team decided to set up a short-term action team with campus volunteers to set some achievable goals that could be widely publicized. In addition to the short-term action team, several other action teams were established with specific goals and distinct assignments over the next several years. Over 180 people volunteered to serve on these teams. After the action teams met their goals, they dissolved, which in and of itself marked progress because the goals were met. This approach differed from the tradition of standing committees that continue to meet without clear progress toward any goals. In addition, the sheer numbers of participants in the roundtables and in the college's faculty and staff development program were also important visible markers of progress.

STAFF DEVELOPMENT

For an institution to do things differently, individuals working within them must also change their behaviors, learn new skills, and develop new capacities. Supporting this personal development has institutional implications. Thus, we learned that staff development played an essential role in transformation. As the examples in this section demonstrate, staff development varied tremendously by institution. Staff and faculty development was offered by centralized administrative offices, by decentralized administrative offices, and by departments or subunits. Some campuses offered development programs across these levels, whereas others targeted strategic groups for training. The decision of how many programs to offer (and how often) was usually tied to the nature of the change initiative. A few campuses chose to have general workshops on the change process, and others offered more general sessions on leadership. Sunshine, Civic State, and Archdiocese institutionalized staff development opportunities beyond the immediate needs created by the change. Middle State, Midwest, and Metropolitan all used approaches that could be modified easily as their change agendas evolved. Finally, leaders made a variety of choices to offer programs either campuswide or targeted to specific groups.

Middle State University

At Middle State, leaders created extensive faculty development opportunities to promote the use of technology in teaching and learning. As this initiative grew, faculty attendance at workshops designed to assist them in improving teaching through technology reached 1,520 people cumulatively. In the words of one campus member, "All faculty now have access to and take advantage of development opportunities for using technology to enhance classes, to teach distance learning classes, to create new classroom materials, and to re-engineer courses." In addition, 1,032 staff enrolled in workshops over the year. Middle State is truly making a comprehensive and sustained effort to develop people's skills. Several individuals commented on the profound need for staff development within transformational changes such as technology, where actual learning, not just a willingness to adjust, is needed.

Metropolitan University

Metropolitan had a multifaceted and expansive development effort for its faculty and staff that included inviting nationally prominent speakers to campus, developing cross-campus interest groups, holding symposia and workshops, and supporting faculty to attend national conferences. One individual described the success of these initiatives: "Over 150 faculty from the pilot units involved in the new curricular core attended workshops in the first year. Cross campus interest groups were formed that explored specific topics related to implementing the core and provided individuals the opportunities to share similar concerns. These [programs] were enormously popular."

Metropolitan's change leaders thought that development should be tied tightly to each unit's goals as they related to the institution's change initiative. They believed that it was important to expand people's notions about development to include learning that was needed to meet organizational, not just individual, goals, which had been the long-held campus belief about faculty development. One of the most important realizations for Metropolitan was that investing in people earns good will and cooperation, which is exceptionally helpful to advance an institutional agenda and goes beyond simply providing new skills. One person noted: "The good will created by providing people opportunities to learn and grow far exceed what we expected. When people grow, they become much more motivated, committed to the institution, have enthusiasm that is contagious, improved morale, and make better decisions. It is truly remarkable what investment in people leads to."

Midwest College

From the beginning, there was an acknowledgement by Midwest leaders that faculty and staff training would be needed to advance change. Developing new learning opportunities on campus is essential for faculty and

staff to develop programs and modify pedagogies to place social responsibility at the heart of their efforts. In the words of one Midwest administrator, "Meaningful and enduring change requires deeper penetration
into the normative systems of the college. A shift from a focus on instruction to learning will require faculty and staff to learn new roles and responsibilities. They will need extensive training and support."

One high-profile strategy adopted at Midwest was to provide opportunities to send all faculty and staff to the Covey Leadership Center to
learn its "Seven Habits of Highly Effective People." A large percentage
of employees took advantage of the opportunity, which was made possible
through a partnership between the institution and the center. In addition,
campus leaders brought Stephen Covey to campus to share his insights
and to develop enthusiasm for the change process.

Nonetheless, at Midwest, the smallest of the six transforming institutions, much of the staff development took place off-campus, both through
the institution's relationship with the Covey Center and by sending teams
to national and regional conferences. At other times, staff development
was incorporated into other activities, such as campus retreats. Perhaps
this approach was related to the costs of developing these programs as
separate on-campus activities at a small institution.

Archdiocese University

At Archdiocese, a larger campus, staff development was extensive and
multilayered, unlike the one-dimensional and integrated approach at
Midwest. For instance, multiple workshops were held in one year so that
faculty who were teaching the writing-intensive section of courses in their
programs would be prepared. In addition, leaders took advantage of a
regional teaching and learning research center located on campus to train
faculty in interactive teaching techniques. Staff from the institute were
asked to develop assessment tools to help faculty better understand the
success of their teaching. Bringing in an outside group heralded the importance of staff development for the campus, similar to Midwest College's move to bring in Stephen Covey. Outside sources often signal that
the campus is serious because they are allocating greater resources and
going beyond traditional development programs. As one person noted:

The human resources division does not have the expertise needed to provide the
staff development we needed to transform the institution. If we had tried to do
all the development internally, I think we might have faltered in our efforts. It

is not that our HR department is not excellent, but that we needed specific expertise and some of it, especially related to changes with the faculty, was just not going to happen through human resources or even our faculty development committees and divisions. Frankly, it was not just expertise, but the excitement generated by engaging outside groups. They brought new ideas and developed further momentum.

Civic State University

The faculty and staff development efforts at Civic State followed three tracks: Civic State sent people off campus to conferences, it developed on-campus reading groups, and it initiated a variety of faculty development workshops. The first strategy, of sending faculty and staff to national conferences and project meetings, provided important exposure to new ideas and strategies, legitimacy to campus problems as faculty realized they were not alone in addressing them, multiple sources of new learning, relationships to draw on to support the change, confidence to create the change, and comfort from others who were engaged in the same process. Although other campuses used national conferences for staff development, none did so to the extent of Civic State.

Reading groups were a second powerful development strategy. Civic State labeled its approach to change as "scholarly" and created a process of inquiry and investigation that would appeal to faculty members and tap their refined skills and strengths. Reading groups consisted of staff and faculty meeting to read a common set of readings, to critique the arguments, and to discuss their relevance to campus efforts. One campus member described the importance of reading groups: "Many on campus identified leading change as scholarship as the most powerful strategy. Wrestling with ideas, reading the literature, and becoming a content expert in the area we were initiating a change provided people with engagement, confidence, and knowledge. Because this has been so successful, the continued challenge for us has been how to provide this experience for even more faculty on a greater set of issues."

The third strategy involved developing a Center for Academic Excellence that developed an extensive array of ongoing programs for campus faculty. The center's teaching fellows program brought in ten new faculty on three-year contracts to teach in the university's new general education program. One administrator commented on the center's programs: "The new administrative structure established in an organized and visible way the many faculty development offerings including faculty mentoring, administrative briefing series for department chairs, technology institutes, community based and service learning support, assessment activities, portfolio development, dialogues on scholarship reconsidered, and other such initiatives. This was one of the essential elements of our change process."

These various faculty development programs have become part of campus operations. They are a means to institutionalize the change efforts.

Sunshine Community College

At Sunshine, staff development was perhaps the most critical element for facilitating change. There were three major initiatives: transformation workshops, the Leadership Academy, and the discipline enrichment courses. The transformation workshops were held at the beginning of Sunshine's efforts for key faculty and staff. The two-and-a-half-day sessions helped to generate a common understanding of the transformation process, explore the literature on change from education and business, review the recommendations from the roundtables, and determine how best to develop a strategy for moving forward. The sessions were part education about transformation strategies and part education about the initiative, as well as an opportunity to shape the process of moving forward.

The flagship program of the college's faculty and staff development efforts was the Leadership Academy, an effort that provided ongoing professional development opportunities for all employees; the content was shaped by the work of the action teams and the roundtables. The Leadership Academy helped provide people with the skills to communicate more effectively, make decisions, and provide input on the change initiative. After the first three years, 123 courses were offered, and attendance cumulated to 1,237 faculty and staff. This may have been the most extensive development effort of any campus. Because of the popularity and importance of the Leadership Academy to the college, Sunshine purchased a nearby house and converted it into a small conference facility used exclusively for the courses. Another successful program has been the Discipline Enrichment Series, which helps faculty to collaboratively enhance learning within a specific discipline through meetings and seminars with colleagues teaching in the same field but at other campuses of the college. The intent of this program is to discuss similar problems and issues around becoming more student centered as it pertains to each field.

SUMMARY

Transformational change depends on intentional strategies. The five core strategies described here offer the keys to changing the culture and bringing about change that is deep and pervasive and that occurs over time.

The detailed examples illustrate the various ways that these strategies emerged on six different campuses, with varied change agendas, and within different institutional cultures and contexts. From these examples, we anticipate that other change leaders will see aspects of their own campus and more clearly understand the challenges they face and the range of potential actions that may provide solutions.

Although this chapter and chapter 3 described key elements of the transformation process—the five core strategies and the tools for helping people think differently—they alone are not enough to succeed on the complex journey of transformation. The next chapter (chapter 5) discusses additional important supporting strategies and describes the interconnection among them and the five strategies discussed here. In chapter 5, we also explore the important concept of balance as it facilitates transformational change.

CHAPTER

The Multifaceted Process of Transformation

Secondary Strategies, Interconnected Approaches, and Balance

Five-step, or even seven- or ten-step, approaches to transformation simply do not exist. No matter what others suggest in their writings or try to persuade campus leaders when consulting, there is no simple, straightforward approach to this complex journey. Even the five core strategies discussed in chapter 4 are by themselves insufficient to effect transformational change. Most people wish that the transformation process could be described in a few pithy directives, but doing so would only frustrate campus change agents because it would tell only part of the complicated story. Simply hitting the highlights does little to advance transformation in practice other than install a false confidence in campus leaders.

The process of transformation is marked by numerous strategies occurring concurrently. The five core strategies are only part of the picture. The journey of transforming institutions suggests that even when institutions had administrative support, used collaborative leadership, created a flexible vision, provided development opportunities, and created visible action, if they did not effectively tap other strategies to advance change, move ahead on a number of fronts simultaneously, and strike a set of balances throughout the process, they did not accomplish major change. This chapter explores the ways in which transformation is complicated and multifaceted. Although five is an easy number of core strategies to remember, the realities of transformation included an additional fifteen strategies that occurred with lesser frequency and played smaller, but still important, roles in facilitating transformation. The core strategies and these additional strategies were intertwined with one another, overlapping, occurring concurrently, and supporting one another. Transformation does not occur linearly but is marked by complex and interrelated approaches. A final important part of this complicated journey is balance, which we explore at the conclusion of this chapter.

The supporting transformation strategies are as follows:

- Putting issues in a broad context
- Setting expectations and holding people accountable
- Persuasive and effective communication
- Invited participation
- Opportunities to influence results
- New interactions
- Changes in administrative and governance processes
- Moderated momentum
- Supportive structures
- Financial resources
- Incentives
- Long-term orientation
- Connections and synergy
- External factors
- Outside perspectives

SUPPORTING STRATEGIES

Institutions that made progress toward transformation followed much more complex approaches than simply adhering to the five core strategies discussed in chapter 4. Although the core strategies played essential roles, they alone could not effect transformational change. Institutions engaged additional strategies as well. Unlike the core strategies, however, these supporting strategies did not occur as frequently across the transforming institutions nor did they play central roles in effecting transformation. We also observed these strategies at other project institutions that were not transforming but that did make notable progress on their change agendas.

Putting Issues in a Broad Context

Institutions that made progress on change placed the local challenge in a larger context. Campus leaders talked about the challenges as being the same as those facing all of American higher education and framed the issues so they extended beyond the borders of the campus. Instilling an understanding of the ways in which the change initiative is part of the broader context raised its level of importance and made the challenges more legitimate. The challenges were no longer simply contrived by campus leaders. Leaders could point to examples of other institutions (frequently, ones that were more prestigious) struggling with similar issues. Campus leaders also drew on the rationales and arguments made by others outside the institution about why a particular challenge is important. Statements made by outsiders often carried more weight on campus than similar statements made internally. Finally, placing change in the larger context helped to depersonalize the issue, making it more palatable to the institution. Leaders could demonstrate that the proposed changes were not an attack on a particular campus subgroup, such as the humanities faculty or the admissions office, but part of a larger trend that transcended any one part of the institution. For example, both Sunshine and Civic State used articles about higher education to put their challenges in a broader context. Sunshine also tapped its external connections with local businesses to help raise the legitimacy of focusing on student learning.

Setting Expectations and Holding People Accountable

Institutional leaders articulated two types of expectations publicly. The first set of expectations concerned the objectives they hoped to accomplish and the ways in which the institution would be not only be different but also better. Leaders realized that key constituencies, before committing to undertaking any particular change, must believe that the proposed change will address something they consider important.

The second set of expectations addressed campus behavior and priorities. Taking the form of a code, guidelines, policies, or a formal or informal statement to the community, these expectations set a direction and provided a framework for action. Rarely was either type of expectation set by a small cadre of administrators working alone. Instead, the expectations were developed through extensive consultation and listening. Campus change leaders, both faculty and administrators, in concert with various campus subgroups, sought to make explicit beliefs that were floating just below the surface. Once articulated, change leaders sought extensive agreement on these beliefs. With explicit and agreed-upon expectations, leaders then used these frameworks to hold individuals and units accountable. For example, leaders at Metropolitan University used an agreed-upon set of goals regarding general education as a template to set expectations and hold individual colleges accountable. At Midwest College, change leaders used the compact they created that outlined behaviors and priorities as a document to hold departments and individuals, including students, accountable.

Persuasive and Effective Communication

"Communicate, communicate, communicate" became a mantra among many institutional leaders during their change efforts. Extensive and even communication rarely happens naturally on most campuses, even at small colleges. Institutions that made significant progress on their change agendas developed extensive internal communication plans. Leaders at Metropolitan called their communication strategy an "intentional on-campus publicity campaign." Change leaders developed a range of strategies to communicate with the campus because they realized that a single communication strategy would not be sufficient. Leaders tapped existing communication venues, such as campus newspapers and periodicals, or regularly scheduled meetings, such as at dean's councils or academic senates, to deliver important information. For example, Middle State created a column in its newspaper called *Technology Bytes*. Institutions also developed new communication outlets to transmit important messages and keep the campus well informed of key decisions. In some instances, these new strategies were campuswide newsletters or Web pages, such as at Sunshine and Metropolitan, devoted to the change initiatives and that gave periodic updates or addressed pertinent issues. Archdiocese sent broadcast e-mails campuswide to inform the campus of its debates and conclusions at least once a month. Other times, institutions released task force reports or white papers that provided more comprehensive information. Midwest released public reports at each stage of its transformation efforts and created a publication called *Midwest Notes* to communicate with key constituents between major reports. Often the release of these task force reports was coupled with attention-grabbing events such as campuswide retreats and visits by nationally eminent speakers.

Invited Participation

Common wisdom about academic change suggests that "involvement" is essential. We learned from the experiences of project institutions that involvement does not simply occur naturally; leaders must invite people to participate and must create diverse opportunities for them. In some instances, institutional leaders developed formal processes for inviting participation, issuing personalized invitations. Other times, leaders used more general requests for input and calls for participation. Change agents invited people to participate in focus groups and retreats and to sit on task forces and advisory bodies. They requested the involvement of whole departments or campus units, asking for written feedback on proposed changes or for comments on draft documents.

Change leaders intentionally structured a range of opportunities to be involved that fit the diverse needs, interests, and availability of faculty, staff, and students. Leaders realized that the term *involvement* does not mean the same thing to everyone. They learned that people could not participate equally (nor did they want to). Some institutions struggled because they invited participation without paying attention to what this truly entailed, creating numerous problems for themselves. Those leaders did not understand that for some people, participation simply means keeping informed of and periodically responding to draft documents, whereas for others on the same campus, participation means having a seat at the decision-making table. Institutions that made progress found ways to tease out these implicit assumptions regarding participation. They invited people to participate in ways that best suited individuals' needs, expectations, and desires.

Finally, change leaders recognized that tapping the expertise, knowledge, and skills of certain individuals on campus could strengthen their efforts. They found ways to extend personal invitations to those key people and ensure their participation. These individuals did not always participate willingly. Frequently, the people needed to contribute significantly to the change process were extremely busy with institutional and professional commitments. They were the distinguished university professors at one campus, the internationally known scholars at another, and the faculty most engaged in advising students beyond their teaching responsibilities at another. Identifying these essential leaders was one thing; getting them to accept an invitation to participate was another, which required persistence as well as good persuasion skills.

Opportunities to Influence Results

Involvement has two components. The first is participation, as just discussed; the second is the opportunity to influence results. At institutions that made progress on their change agendas, participants in the transformation process were able to see their influence on its course and outcomes. Seeing the fruits of one's labor increased individuals' commitment to the change process, created a sense of confidence and accomplishment in shaping institution-wide initiatives (something many faculty working independently in their departments had not experienced), and ultimately, improved the process. On the other hand, inviting participation with limited results deterred rather than advanced change. People who believed that their time and energy were not appreciated or taken seriously by change leaders quickly became disheartened. In some instances, these individuals opted out of the change process completely; in others, they became active opponents to the proposed changes. At Sunshine and Midwest, for example, faculty who submitted comments on draft documents were able to see their language and ideas incorporated into future versions. Leaders at both institutions were careful to summarize the feedback and make it widely available to the institution. In these instances, even if people did not see their ideas in final drafts, they received an acknowledgment of their contributions.

Some of the transforming institutions recognized the importance of this strategy early in their process. They developed a practice of labeling each document with the word *DRAFT*. They continually revisited documents, updating them as appropriate. They also widely circulated all of the comments they received on project documents. These processes allowed a large number of people see their fingerprints on the change.

New Interactions

Institutional leaders brought together in new configurations a variety of campus subgroups and individuals. Leaders recognized that people fall into routines and that by breaking them, campus members will interact with new people in different ways. Taking people outside of well-worn roles helped spark the creative thinking and approaches needed during change. At some institutions, these approaches brought together people who had never met but shared similar concerns, creating new cohorts interested in taking on difficult issues. Metropolitan used this strategy in its cross-college interest groups. The roundtables and action teams at Sunshine illustrate this point. Changing the composite of groups led to different dynamics, new conversations, and the exchange of ideas. At other institutions, leaders learned that sometimes simply reconvening the usual suspects under different circumstances and at a different location and time led to new behavior.

Bringing people together in new ways helped foster communication across the campus. It also helped instill a greater sense of trust, clear up potential misunderstandings and rumors, and create a sense of community. By making personal connections and interacting on a regular basis, people in different campus subgroups came to see the range of perspectives operating in the same institution. They learned that their assumptions about other people were not always correct (such as scientists' views of faculty in professional programs or student affairs professionals' views of various groups of faculty). Finally, these interactions helped instill a sense that they are all "in this together." No longer was each group going it alone; they were part of a larger community facing the same challenges, a point particularly important at institutions such as Sunshine with its four campuses and at Metropolitan with its autonomous colleges.

Changes in Administrative and Governance Processes

Institutions made a range of alterations to administrative processes to support the changes. The intent behind this modification in campus decision processes was to ensure that the changes became part of the day-to-day business within departmental, college, and division activities. These changes reflected new institutional priorities and helped in many ways to facilitate the transformation agenda. There was not a particular set of administrative alterations across project institutions; it all depended on the circumstances of the institution and its particular change agenda. Some campuses realized they might need to establish a new center, divide units, reconfigure roles, and the like. For example, Archdiocese and Middle State both changed the way they purchased new computer software. No longer would each institution allow individual units to make their own purchases unless highly specialized. By centralizing the purchasing function, leaders could bring together faculty who rarely interacted, such as faculty in different departments that all taught statistics, under the auspices of reaching consensus and recommending a common campus software package. These meetings resulted in new conversations among faculty about teaching and learning based on software recommendations.

Institutions also tinkered with governance processes to facilitate change. Transformational change requires that leaders pay close attention to governance processes such as faculty and academic senates, joint faculty-administrator committees, student government, and the board and its committees. Institutional leaders recognized the ways in which current governance structures could facilitate change, as well as the limitations within structures that could hinder change. Those institutions that made progress on transformation were not afraid to create new ad hoc campus decision-making groups. Institutional leaders made sure that these new bodies adhered to well-accepted norms of legitimacy or else they risked derailing the change process over questions of governance. In many instances, these new groups could work faster than standing governance committees or could make decisions in new areas that fell outside traditional committee structures.

Moderated Momentum

Another important strategy was the intentional moderation of the pace of change. Too much change quickly could overwhelm or exhaust the institution, creating a backlash against the change process, as Sunshine realized. Too little progress and the change agenda might stall, as Civic State learned. The change agenda could easily fall off the institution's collective radar screen, change leaders could become disheartened with their lack of progress, naysayers could point to the futility of the change, and the change agenda risks being replaced by one that can be more easily accomplished. Leaders in all instances refrained from forcing issues when they thought that insistence would result in hasty decisions or would alienate those individuals whose cooperation would later be needed. To moderate the pace of change, leaders controlled the number and type of decisions being made and the timetable for departments and individuals to respond and react to documents or implement accepted changes in policy. They paced the release of reports and the visits of outsiders to campus. They created plans to intentionally roll out various phases of the change and particular initiatives. Being intentional about the pace of change is different from micromanaging the change process. Leaders in all instances worked to find an optimal rate for change; however, they did not seek to influence the outcomes of the processes, instead favoring the recommendations and insights of the campus.

Supportive Structures

In addition to altering existing administrative structures, new structures often needed to be added to campus operations. Change leaders at the transforming institutions recognized that change does not simply happen unsupported. They realized that change depends on a variety of structures to facilitate change. In some cases, these new structures included creating a new position to oversee a particular part of the change effort or giving key faculty leaders release time or administrative support. In other instances, institutions created new units such as centers for teaching excellence, computer support offices, or offices responsible for university-community relations. These new positions and offices not only showed that someone was responsible for the issues surrounding the change but also sent the message that these issues were important enough to receive staff, budgets, and office space.

Financial Resources

Institutional leaders provided financial resources to support part of the transformation agenda. They found new sources of revenue and reallocated existing funds. Without adequate financial support, good ideas simply withered on the vine. Leaders at Archdiocese University tapped its quasi-endowment to support the creation of the technology infrastructure essential to their transformation efforts. Metropolitan and Midwest secured large investments from foundations. Middle State University obtained one-time state funds to support its transformation efforts, and Sunshine obtained federal Title III funds to underwrite some of its work. In addition to providing needed resources to pay for new initiatives, the additional funds created a sense of legitimacy for the changes, particularly when the monies came from gifts and grants. Faculty and staff saw these funds as recognition and appreciation of their hard work.

Incentives

Financial resources helped create incentives at transforming institutions. These campuses used a range of incentives, including summer salaries, computer upgrades, conference travel, and public recognition, to motivate key individuals to commit time and energy to the change process. Incentives were used not only to encourage new behavior and priorities but also to recognize those individuals and units that were already doing things consistent with the change agenda. Leaders at Middle State encouraged departments to expand their promotion and tenure policies to include different forms of scholarship. Frequently, the campuswide recognition was more important than the award. Incentives, and their announcement and use, helped keep the priorities of the change agenda on individuals' and departments' radar screens.

Long-Term Orientation

Transformation is a long-term endeavor. Savvy institutional leaders recognize this and plan their approaches to effecting change accordingly by developing strategies that capture and hold the campus's collective attention through many distractions and over years, not months. For many leaders, this means spending time laying the groundwork for change, taking necessary steps to build credibility and trust prior to engaging the campus in the challenging work of transformation. Recognizing and planning for change over the long term requires different assumptions and strategies than change made more quickly. Leaders at Sunshine extended their strategies and timetable once they realized that their intended change would take more than two to three years. They created a set of faculty and staff development opportunities because they understood that the change would need to be sustained over time and that a series of workshops and professional development opportunities would keep college attention on the key issues over time and would also give people access to knowledge and skills that would sustain the efforts. By expanding their time frame, they were able to fit these activities into their efforts.

Campus leaders must weigh the short- and long-term consequences of particular change strategies and abandon those that can potentially derail the change effort later in the process. Many campus leaders chose not to fight some battles and to modify other approaches and time frames to accommodate the long-term nature of transformation. For example, the president and provost at Midwest knew that they could write a new mission and value statement quickly. However, rather than foisting their version on the campus, they designed a process that took much longer and was more inclusive to draft these statements. They realized that the short-term gain of their own statement could have long-term consequences that would prevent transformation from occurring.

Connections and Synergy

A key to successful change for many institutions was finding and creating linkages among various activities on and off campus that helped campuses create and sustain the energy necessary for transformation. On many campuses, new energy was created because multiple projects facilitated new connections among individuals from different parts of the institution. At other places, connections reassured people that they were not working in isolation; this knowledge helped push people along. Institutions created connections through cross-departmental teams and through common tasks that leaders could charge to a particular working group, including drafting documents, representing the institution at conferences, giving presentations, and conducting campus assessments.

Institutions built additional important linkages with organizations and individuals outside the institution. For example, Midwest, Sunshine, and Civic State found ways to join national projects, such as those run by the American Association for Higher Education, Harvard University, The League for Innovation, and the Carnegie Foundation for the Advancement of Teaching, to advance their efforts at home. Through connections to funding agencies, other colleges and universities, and national projects and associations, institutions leveraged outside experts, energy, and interest to promote change internally. These external connections added another layer of legitimacy to the change efforts and helped generate important momentum for the efforts. Understanding how issues at a particular institution are connected to others outside helps overcome insularity that impeded movement. The outside audiences provided opportunities to test ideas with neutral audiences, learn from others' experiences and mistakes, develop new solutions, and create supportive networks.

External Factors

Leaders at transforming institutions constructively used events and activities outside the institution to promote change internally, such as legislative actions, economic opportunities or downturns, the local business community, and foundation priorities to advance their on-campus efforts. They looked at calls for proposals and conference announcements as opportunities. These elements provided an important external context that helped provide legitimacy, confirmed beliefs and assumptions, and provided needed money and support. They also helped the institution reflect on its progress and develop concrete action plans, articulate its beliefs and assumptions to outside audiences, and become more attuned to changes in the environment that could either facilitate or hamper their efforts.

Outside Perspectives

External linkages also help institutions tap outsiders' perspectives that could advance change on campus. Finding ways to incorporate and explore ideas and assumptions different from the prevailing ones on campus helps institutions reconceptualize their processes. Transforming institutions benefited from new ways of thinking, as well as from comments, suggestions, and challenges that surfaced unexplored assumptions and beliefs. Outsiders, in many instances, can ask questions that would have been difficult for campuses to raise. Often, institutions invited external experts to campus. Other times, institutions sent teams of faculty and administrators to visit other institutions and to attend national and regional meetings and conferences. At all of the transforming institutions, leaders widely distributed key readings and developed ways to discuss those readings at retreats, during regularly scheduled meetings, or through reading groups, organized as professional development seminars specifically designed to explore new ideas.

INTERRELATED APPROACHES

The traditional change literature frequently describes change processes as occurring through a series of steps: for example, (1) craft a vision, (2) develop a plan, (3) communicate the vision and secure buy-in, (4) find the necessary resources, and so on. These processes typically are described as discrete tasks. Developing a plan has little to do with the creation of incentives, except once the plan is ready to be implemented. We learned that change does not occur in a linear stepwise fashion, nor are change strategies distinct from one another. Instead, transformation is composed of interrelated strategies that build upon and reinforce one another.

As already discussed, institutions that advanced their transformation agendas engaged five core strategies and fifteen supporting strategies. Twenty strategies to remember and engage the institution seem like a very complex undertaking. However, these twenty strategies are not always accomplished as discrete tasks. One does not have to generate senior administrative support, then undertake staff development, after which one invites participation, brings in outside perspectives, and then provides incentives. Campus change leaders found ways to connect strategies and devise approaches that satisfied multiple objectives. Institutions embarked on activities that frequently accounted for more than one strategy. The five core strategies tend to be nodes to which other strategies linked. The number and variety of interconnected strategies varied by the activities or approaches developed by each institution. However, not all activities served multiple strategies. This section illustrates some of the ways in which the transformation strategies are interrelated.

Senior Administrative Support

The activities and approaches that were linked to senior administrative support included (1) changes in administrative and governance processes,

(2) external factors, (3) support structures, (4) incentives, and (5) financial resources. As previously noted, senior administrators were able to engage a set of strategies that few others at the institution could accomplish. Their vested authority held them responsible for fiduciary matters and decision making on campus. Many of the support strategies related to senior administrative support concerned these two areas, fiduciary (incentives, financial resources, support structures) or decision making (administrative and governance structures, external factors). We draw upon a few examples to illustrate these relationships.

At Middle State, senior administrators played important roles in initiating and sustaining the transformation agenda by positioning the institution to take advantage of incentive funding from the state, an external factor. According to one person on campus, the president was in "a position to read what the legislature was interested in funding" and "took advantage of this edge early; the change process . . . would not have come about as quickly if MSU had not tapped into the resources when they were first available." This activity demonstrates that beyond providing senior administrative support, the president was able to leverage outside factors to provide financial support that he then leveraged into internal incentives.

At Midwest, it was the president who communicated the work of the faculty-led Vision Commission to the board and obtained their buy-in. He also organized the follow-up campuswide retreat and charged the faculty with exploring the student learning outcomes of the newly adopted vision. Through his actions, he tapped external factors (the board) and invited participation both in the retreat and in the Learning Outcomes Group. Through the newly formed, faculty-led Learning Outcomes Group, the president provided a mechanism for faculty to influence results. Finally, he worked to keep the momentum flowing by creating this new mechanism after the board retreat, realizing that the campus could view board approval as a final step. By charging the Learning Outcomes Group, he kept the process moving forward.

Collaborative Leadership

Institutions linked collaborative leadership with the supporting strategies of (1) invited participation, (2) opportunities to influence results, (3) support structures, (4) new interactions, and (5) communication. Collaboration entails a set of strategies focused on the human element or dynamic. Interaction, communication, and participation are all critical subcomponents of collaborative leadership.

At Sunshine Community College, as part of the 1997 faculty welcome back events, the change leaders provided a forum for all interested faculty to hear and react to the reports that were written over the summer by the institution's four action teams. Approximately three hundred faculty and staff attended the event. The retreat sponsors organized the participants into small groups for discussion. To deliver consistent messages from the four action teams, the campus change leaders showed each small group a videotape of the team delivering its report. All participants received written copies of each report as well. The small groups discussed the reports and ideas presented by the action teams. Their comments were recorded and compiled into a feedback report that was shared not only with the action teams but campuswide. This approach illustrates some of the supporting strategies connected to collaborative leadership. The change leaders put a spotlight on collaborative leadership illustrated by the work of the four action teams. They invited participation to the retreat, and by compiling and widely disseminating the feedback they made transparent the opportunity to influence results by shaping the recommendations to the action teams. The videotape and the written reports were intentional strategies to communicate the work of the teams clearly and consistently to small groups of faculty and staff.

Staff Development

Often staff development was linked to (1) outside perspectives, (2) communication, and (3) connections and synergy. For example, at Civic State University, leaders developed a campuswide retreat to focus on faculty work for the twenty-first century. The morning consisted of plenary sessions, some of which included outside speakers. The afternoon sessions were organized into small discussion groups to react to the speakers' messages. The morning agenda tapped the different ideas of outsiders, whereas the afternoon session helped facilitate cross-departmental conversations, creating new connections around issues of common interest.

As part of its transformation efforts, Sunshine Community College launched the Discipline Enrichment Series, a set of activities intended to bring together faculty teaching in the same fields from all four campuses of the college. Although Sunshine is a single institution, the faculty are connected much more tightly to one of the four campuses. Thus, faculty who teach mathematics at one campus in most instances had never interacted with the mathematics faculty at the other three campuses. The Discipline Enrichment Series was unique because it was college-wide, rather than campus specific. The focus of the series was to help faculty develop major-specific strategies that would ensure student success. This approach not only helped give faculty new ideas, knowledge, and skills but also made important new connections across the college and created new avenues of communication across campus boundaries.

At Midwest College, the leadership created a speaker series that brought to campus local, national, and international speakers to address topics related to civic engagement and social responsibility. All faculty, staff, and students were invited to attend the lectures as professional development opportunities. The speakers, representing a diverse set of experiences and organizations, helped the institution think more broadly about its agreed-upon ideas. Midwest also arranged for all of its employees to participate in an off-site leadership training institute at the Covey Leadership Center to learn about the skills of highly effective people. This strategy not only provided leadership training for a range of employees; it introduced the campus on an extensive scale to a set of outside principles and ideas as its members developed their abilities and skills.

Flexible Vision

Strategies such as (1) outside perspectives, (2) long-term orientation, (3) communication, (4) momentum, (5) putting issues in a broader context, (6) connections, and (7) setting expectations became connected with the core strategy of flexible vision.

For example, Archdiocese University developed a structure and process to help academic units redesign key courses to be technology intensive. Rather than prescribe how departments were to adopt technology into their courses, the institution created the Curricular Development Program (CDP), an annual internal grants competition, to allow good ideas to emerge from the faculty. The program does not specify specific projects, but it does provide a set of parameters for proposed initiatives. The guidelines for suggested proposals should "provide significant, valuable, and pedagogically innovative curricula. CDP encourages proposals that address cross-disciplinary issues, focus on courses with high enrollments, and chart a thoughtful study and thorough assessment of such initiatives." This initiative is broadly structured to encourage a range of creative thinking that yields a flexible plan without dictating a particular strategy or foreclosing ideas that might emerge across campus. Its parameters set expectations and reinforce certain behaviors as the criteria and the winners are widely communicated across campus. Its cross-disciplinary nature encourages connections and synergy across programs. A single department cannot submit a proposal. The project is ongoing, having begun in

1996; thus it has a long-term effect on the institution as each year's projects generate more widespread innovation. Each year's winners build on the work of others and generate more innovations across campus building momentum. Finally, this highly visible program sets campuswide expectations of good practice through its criteria and announcements of chosen projects.

Taking Visible Action

We observed that taking visible action was linked to supporting strategies such as (1) supportive structures, (2) communication, (3) setting expectations and holding people accountable, (4) connections and synergy, (5) financial resources, and (6) incentives.

One set of activities common across many of the transforming institutions that brought together taking visible action with other support strategies was retreats. At Midwest College, the campus designed a series of retreats that brought together the campus community to discuss key issues, learn about progress to date, and provide opportunities to respond to proposed courses of action and documents. At Sunshine Community College, change leaders used periodic roundtable conversations open to the campus as a whole. At Civic State, leaders incorporated campuswide conversations about their transformation efforts into annual faculty convocations and into ongoing faculty development activities. Each of these approaches provided highly visible opportunities for faculty and staff to see campus progression on its transformation agenda. At the same time, leaders invited participation, brought people together to create new connections and synergy, and used the retreats as prime opportunities for communication. Change leaders at each institution intentionally framed the conversations they wanted the campus to hold and used the gatherings as opportunities to provide updates and disseminate other pertinent information.

Beyond retreats, institutions used other approaches to link related strategies. At Middle State University, the drafting and release of the faculty-led report A New Day was an important visible action for the campus. It not only provided an opportunity for faculty to demonstrate important leadership (collaborative leadership), but it also illustrated their ability to influence results and incorporate outside perspectives as the document drew heavily upon Boyer's extended definitions of scholarship.

At Civic State University, the building of new classroom space specifically for use by classes in the new general education program was an important milestone that illustrated visible action and a range of supporting strategies. These new classrooms were designed specifically for the pedagogies that were driving the new first- and second-year general education courses. Using the latest technology, having flexible seating arrangements, and being located near computer laboratories and student mentor offices, these classrooms were functional for the faculty teaching those courses and also sent important messages about the institution's long-term commitment to the program. This strategy called for significant financial resources and set expectations for student and faculty behavior by its design.

Links between Core Strategies

The core strategies do not tend to be linked as often with one another as with supporting strategies. However, two examples are worth discussing. The first is staff development and collaborative leadership. We saw that unless there is a common understanding about the change process and the nature of the change, communication is hampered, collaborative leadership suffers, and other difficulties arise. An important part of developing and sustaining collaborative leadership is providing people throughout the institution the skills, knowledge, and perspectives needed to fulfill those responsibilities. The second is senior administrative support and collaborative leadership. Senior administrative support enables collaborative leadership in most instances. Most individuals on campus did not believe that the process of leading the change initiative was collaborative unless senior administrative staff invited participation and empowered committees. Without the blessing of senior administrators, collaborative leadership would not work effectively to advance change. Instead, it would clash with senior administrators over who leads change and which agenda gets advanced.

One last point can be made on the interconnected nature of transformation strategies. We learned from the institutions' experiences that not all strategies are connected—some supporting strategies tended to cluster with specific core strategies whereas others did not. For example, we did not find examples of long-term orientation, influencing results, or invited participation connected with the core strategy of taking visible action, nor did we see changes in administration and governance linked with collaborative leadership or staff development. So although many strategies are interdependent, not all are directly linked.

BALANCE

The final element that is critical to the transformation process is balance. With twenty interrelated strategies and a long-term effort to effect transformation that is both deep and pervasive, transforming institutions discovered the importance of striking numerous balances in their change efforts. Previously discussed was the supporting strategy to moderate the pace of change that required leaders to balance speed with patience. Likewise, we discovered other types of balance that leaders struck that were central to transformation. What needs to be balanced depends on the institution, its culture, and its change agenda. That said, the experiences of transforming institutions suggest some common types of balance.

Institutions learned of the importance of balancing participation in many ways. They found that to keep their institutions on track, they had to find ways to keep a diversity of faculty involved. If the process was seen as driven only by faculty from the sciences or from the professional schools, for example, trouble could emerge. Somewhat through trial and error, and based on an understanding of their cultures, institutions learned that on occasion, they had to find the balance between junior and seasoned faculty, between faculty from different disciplines, and between faculty who teach predominately undergraduates and those in the graduate school. Institutions also had to find ways to balance faculty and staff participation, and sometimes with student involvement. Too many participants from any one group could easily tip the scales and derail the change process.

Institutions that made progress on their transformation agendas struck a workable balance between internal and external perspectives and involvement. Too many ideas from inside the campus led to an insularity that was difficult to break. Too many outside voices created a process that faculty and staff had difficulty feeling that they owned. However, the internal-external balance that worked for institutions differed. For example, Sunshine Community College, which historically had strong connections to its local community, used outside voices more frequently than did Metropolitan University, which had a strong tradition of faculty autonomy. And Civic State had to redefine its workable balance between inside and outside perspectives as its change agenda—to become an urban university—evolved.

Finding ways to create short-term gains while laying the groundwork for long-term needs proved to be another important type of balance. For instance, Sunshine institutionalized this balance with its short-term action committees. Its leaders realized that without visible markers of success, the institution would grow impatient with the change process. At

Midwest College, leaders found ways to ensure immediate results while planting the seeds needed for transformation over the long term. They used the periodic retreats to inform the campus of recent progress, and they found ways to break up the major elements of their change agenda into discrete tasks that could be undertaken sequentially. For example, they set out to first articulate a new vision and then identify learning outcomes for that vision. They then looked into a range of new pedagogies that would generate the proposed learning outcomes.

Finally, institutions balanced the new and the old. For some institutions embarking on major change, the idea of transformation was overwhelming. Faculty and staff were worried that leaders were trying to create a completely different institution and that transformation meant a condemnation of their work and personal and professional commitments. Others worried that transformation would negate the characteristics that made their institution special. To accommodate these concerns, institutional leaders found ways to reinforce, and in many cases celebrate, long-held beliefs or programs and at the same time challenge the institution to do new things. They stressed new priorities and reinforced existing mission, values, goals, and priorities that were to remain unchanged. For example, Midwest College turned to its original founding documents to strike this balance. The leaders asked the institution how it could reconfigure the undergraduate experience to provide students with "the means of intellectual, moral, and spiritual improvement and to teach them the Divine art and science of doing good to others," which is a passage from an early college catalogue, dated 1846. Even at institutions that were clear about undertaking transformation, leaders made it widely known that they were not throwing out the baby with the bath water.

CONCLUSION

Transformational change is not a straightforward task. As this chapter illustrates, being successful requires a complex process and demands that leaders consider a range of strategies and activities. We noted twenty different strategies, the ways in which some are interrelated, and the need to balance many factors as institutions move forward. As we proclaimed at the outset, transformation is difficult.

That said, our complication of the journey of transformation is not yet finished. The next chapter explores the ways in which particular institutional cultures shape the process of transformation. Without adhering to cultural norms, expectations, and preferences, the core and secondary strategies—no matter how many are used or which balances are struck—will not yield desired results.

CHAPTER 6

Making Strategies Unique

Institutional Culture

The relationship between institutional culture and transformational change is important.[1] Yet it is not a readily recognizable part of the transformation process. Most higher education leaders are aware that colleges and universities have distinctive cultures that shape and help define key institutional features such as faculty autonomy, academic excellence, academic freedom, student subcultures, and campus social ethos. Each institution has a particular culture that helps define what it is, how it operates, and what is does (Kuh & Whitt, 1988; Schein, 1992). For many campus leaders getting a firm grasp on their own institutional culture is difficult because they are immersed in it. Campus leaders tend to understand the nuances of their culture clearly only after the change process violates important parts of it, such as what it truly means to "involve" the faculty. Institutional culture plays an important role in bringing about transformational change as well as impeding its progress when violated. This chapter begins by reviewing key ideas about institutional culture and explains the two cultural frameworks that shaped our understanding. We follow this discussion with a description of three of the six transforming institutions and describe the way institutional culture affected their change processes.

INSTITUTIONAL CULTURE

The idea of institutional culture has entered the everyday campus lexicon. However, its frequent use means that many of the nuances of the concept have been glossed over. Early scholarship on culture in higher education explored the distinctive cultures at individual institutions that strongly differentiated them from other types of institutions, such as Reed or Bennington Colleges. The thinking that frames this chapter, although acknowledging that special campuses exist as identified by that early scholarship, suggests that each institution has its own culture that in some key ways makes it behave uniquely. Yet, all institutions of higher education share, at the same time, a common academic culture that makes lessons such as those offered in this book widely applicable.

Culture is defined as "the deeply embedded patterns of organizational behavior and the shared values, assumptions, beliefs, or ideologies that members have about their organization or its work" (Peterson & Spencer, 1991, p. 142). Culture provides meaning and sets the context for people in a specific organization (Bergquist, 1992; Schein, 1992). A survey of the literature revealed the following elements associated with the concept of culture: (1) norms or specific guides that shape conduct, (2) agreed-upon values espoused throughout an organization, (3) the philosophy that guides the campus's attitudes, understandings, priorities, and actions regarding students, staff, faculty, and teaching, research, and service (Kuh & Whitt, 1988). We use these elements to frame this chapter.

As noted in chapter 2, these elements can be organized and understood as a set of layers. The top layer is most visible and includes the key artifacts that help define the institution, such as planning documents, institutional structures, and policies. The second layer, more difficult to detect, includes the values and ideals espoused by the campus, such as being learning centered or valuing diversity. The third layer is composed of the underlying assumptions and are the deeply held and rarely examined institutional beliefs, such as what it means to be a teaching institution (Schein, 1992). Culture is ubiquitous throughout campus processes and structures. It influences elements such as mission, leadership, information dissemination and communication, strategic planning, and the socialization of new members (Tierney, 1991). Yet it is this ubiquity that makes it difficult to discern for the people within an institution who encounter it everyday and thus difficult to tap effectively to advance transformational change.

Understanding one's own institutional culture is important to the transformation process, as this chapter demonstrates. One cannot have transformational change without altering at least some aspects of institutional culture. It also is easy to imagine that the culture of an institution, being a fundamental aspect of the organization, would influence the processes the institution uses to affect change. This second relationship causes the most trouble for campus change leaders working to bring about transformation because many pay little attention to the ways in which culture shapes their intentional change strategies and processes. When efforts fail, there is the plethora of excuses or blame. Typical responses include, "Faculty do not want to change," "The institution lacks the money for incentives," "We are simply too complex and large to move forward," and "The board doesn't support our ideas." Rarely does anyone ever say, "We forgot to follow our institutional culture." Leaders rarely want to admit that some characteristics of their own institution (whether hidden or overt) tripped them up.

The experiences of the transforming institutions suggest that culture plays an important role not only as something that is changed as a result of transformation but also as a key factor in the transformation process. Two links between culture and change traditionally have been made in the higher education literature. The first set suggests that institutions need to have a "culture" that encourages change (see, for example, Curry, 1992). The goal of this body of research is to determine the aspects or type of culture that need to be fostered to promote institutional change. The second set of ideas suggests that culture, or key institutional elements that shape culture—such as vision or mission—are modified as a result of the change process (Chaffee & Tierney, 1988; Guskin, 1996). In other words, the outcome of change is a modified culture (Schein, 1992). We suggest a third path, important for leaders to understand the way their institution's culture shapes change processes or strategies. The culture is the modifying element rather than the subject of the modification. The experiences of project institutions suggest that leaders must learn to take their institutional culture, in addition to the type of change and the substance of their change agenda, into consideration. Understanding one's institutional culture requires that leaders examine the fit between how they are going about the change process and making sure it is consistent with the artifacts, values, and assumptions that shape the institution and its processes. This chapter demonstrates how leaders at three transforming institutions took their cultures into consideration and used them wisely to shape their change processes as they embarked on transformation.

FRAMEWORKS FOR UNDERSTANDING INSTITUTIONAL CULTURE

Because culture is such a complex aspect of campus and often difficult for people in the midst of it to interpret, tools are needed to guide change agents in their efforts toward transformation. We chose two frameworks as guides to help leaders understand the way culture influences the change process. The first was Bergquist's institutional archetypes of culture; the second was Tierney's unique institutional culture.

Bergquist's (1992) book *The Four Cultures of the Academy* identifies four types of cultures (archetypes) by which numerous institutions can be categorized and described. (Please refer to the book for a more detailed discussion of the four cultures.) He hypothesized (yet never empirically tested) that different change strategies would be needed and appropriate within the four different academic cultures—the collegial culture, the managerial culture, the developmental culture, and the negotiating culture. The *collegial culture* arises primarily from the disciplines of the faculty. It values scholarly engagement, shared governance and decision making, and rationality. The *managerial culture* focuses on the goals and purposes of the institution, and it values efficiency, effective supervisory skills, and fiscal responsibility. This contrasts with the *developmental culture*, which is based on the personal and professional growth of all members of the collegiate environment. Finally, the *negotiating culture* prizes the establishment of equitable and egalitarian policies and procedures, valuing confrontation, interest groups, mediation, and power. Bergquist illustrated how the managerial culture, for example, might hinder an institution's ability to change structures, whereas a collegial culture was better equipped to modify institutional structures because there was greater trust.

Although Bergquist's framework provides one lens for examining the effect of institutional culture on change strategies, these institutional cultural archetypes can mask many of the complexities of individual institutional cultures, which led us to adopt Tierney's (1991) framework as the means to explore the ways in which culture affects change processes within individual institutions. The Tierney framework includes the following six categories: environment, mission, socialization, information, strategy, and leadership. He suggests a cultural analysis that consists of examining each category in depth, asking questions such as the following: How is the mission defined and articulated? Is it used as a basis for decisions? What constitutes information, and who has it? How are decisions arrived at, and who makes them? This approach assumes that the values, beliefs, and assumptions of an institution are reflected in its processes and artifacts.

As we noted earlier when describing the three levels of institutional culture, the outer layer of artifacts is the most easily discovered. Thus, our analysis focuses primarily on the artifacts. We then used these to begin unearthing the deeper values and underlying assumptions.

By examining the key elements suggested by both Bergquist and Tierney, we developed a clearer picture of the institutional culture and its effect on transformation processes. When both frameworks are used together, they provide a more powerful lens than using only one in helping to interpret and understand culture and transformation. Bergquist's archetypes provide a ready framework for institutions unfamiliar with cultural analysis by establishing patterns for them to identify. The Tierney lens provides a sophisticated tool for understanding the complexities of unique institutions. The dual level of analysis offers a multiple-lens perspective better suited to understand complex organizational phenomenon (Birnbaum, 1988; Bolman & Deal, 1991; Eckel, 1998). We used the key principles of each framework to explore the ways in which the five core strategies vary within different institutional cultures. The following list illustrates the way we used Bergquist and Tierney to examine culture and transformation.

Bergquist's Cultural Archetypes	+ Tierney's Individual Institutional Culture	→ Change Strategies
Collegial culture	Environment	Senior administrative support
Managerial culture	Mission	Collaborative leadership
Developmental culture	Socialization	Flexible vision
Negotiating culture	Information	Staff development
	Strategy	Visible actions
	Leadership	

To illustrate the relationship of culture to the change process, we focus on three of the six campuses: Middle State University, Metropolitan University, and Sunshine Community College. For each campus, we first describe the campus culture and then provide an overview of the ways that the institution's change process was distinctive based on its culture, as reviewed through both the Bergquist and Tierney frameworks.

The institutional cultures described in the rest of the chapter were identified through detailed study and analysis of the campus cultures. Please see Appendix B for information about the study methodology. In addition, please see Kezar & Eckel (2002) for more detailed descriptions of campus culture. In brief, data analysis was conducted through three different approaches. First, theme analysis of the change strategies was conducted, examining the ways in which each strategy was enacted at each institution. Second, researchers developed institutional culture profiles of all six institutions based on the Bergquist and Tierney frameworks for examining institutional culture. Third, these frameworks were applied to the data to determine whether institutional culture patterns could be identified in the change strategies. After the analysis was completed, the profiles of institutional culture, change strategies, and the relationship between the two conditions were sent to the site visit researchers (other than the lead researchers) to confirm interpretations of institutional culture and to have outsiders check the themes that emerged.

MIDDLE STATE UNIVERSITY: DEVELOPMENTAL, INFORMAL, AND TRUSTING CULTURE

The culture at Middle State University can be described as developmental, informal, and trusting. At Middle State, both the organizational culture and change strategies used reflect the developmental culture in Bergquist's typology. The mission and faculty socialization strongly supported the importance of learning; recently, the institution defined itself as a "premier teaching university." Bergquist noted that many developmental cultures tend to have a strong focus on teaching. The leadership process on developmental campuses tends to be facilitative and strongly collaborative, which was the case at Middle State. Developmental campuses such as this one also tend to share information widely since it is critical to growth.

Through the Tierney lens, Middle State's culture is best characterized by the terms *informal* and *trusting*. Although a sense of trust is likely to develop within the developmental culture, it is stronger than that described in Bergquist's framework. Trust at Middle State appears to result from the long and stable leadership created by having the same president and provost for more than fifteen years, the large number of long-term dedicated employees (over 60 percent have only worked under the current president and provost), and a strong connection between the campus and its community. The institution also is run exceedingly informally. For example, it does not have a formal strategic planning process; instead, institutional direction is set informally and communicated through a series of conversations between the president, the provost, and various key stakeholders. Middle State's policies and practices tend to be developed locally in departments and colleges, and they were modified frequently, and lacked uniformity. Although some campus decision-making structures are in place, such as a faculty senate, there appears to be little reliance on them as the primary decision-making venues. Much of the business of the campus happens around a lunch table, in the hallways, or through a variety of different meetings. People who work at Middle State are likely to know each other well, interacting both within the workplace and outside of it in the local community.

The Five Core Change Strategies and Middle State's Culture

At Middle State, senior administrative support appeared in the background of the change efforts and primarily consisted of providing needed resources and facilities regarding technology. Senior administrators also continually reminded the campus of the importance of technology and computer competency, but they were laissez-faire in the direction of the initiatives. Middle State differed from the developmental culture in the way senior administrative support emerged; for example, no governance structures were altered or support mechanisms established. Bergquist predicted that leaders within a developmental culture would establish many support mechanisms to facilitate change; governance structures were typically altered to ensure inclusiveness, and formal communication vehicles were typically established. Yet, within Middle State's informal environment, people, not processes or structures, were the core support. Furthermore, the informal communication around lunch tables and in hallways with key campus leaders was the ideal process, rather than the more deliberate communication mechanisms established within typical developmental cultures.

Collaborative leadership was a natural element within the developmental culture of Middle State, where decisions and much of the action was pushed out to individual academics and departments. Mechanisms for collaborative leadership were already established through informal information networks and cross-departmental groups that met on a regular basis to discuss improvements. Developing people's leadership capacities and tapping their creativity had been a long-term philosophy for the current administration. Examining this institution through the lens of their individual cultures, we saw that collaborative leadership was enacted in distinctive ways. The trusting and informal environment of Middle State shaped involvement; campus leaders did not need to invite participation or develop channels for communication, and there was no need to work through troubled relations on campus.

Middle State's developmental culture epitomized the flexibility inherent in the concept of flexible vision. Institutional leaders had no overall grand scheme for change; instead, they established a process launching a series of uncoordinated, yet broadly linked change efforts. Decisions and ideas emerged at the local, departmental level, often informally. The few planning documents that emerged did so within programs and departments and were for local use. The vision and "real" plan for the future regarding technology and the educational experience was the strategy of each department. Even new promotion and tenure criteria that reflected the institution's technology goals was left to the design of each unit to best fit their specific disciplinary contexts. On most campuses with a developmental culture similar to Middle State, a detailed and clear robust. plan would be critical for moving forward with change. Yet, within Middle State's environment of high trust and familiarity, it appears that there was little need for this type of documentation, which was unique to their distinctive culture.

The developmental culture at Middle State, which was heavily tied to the growth of people on campus, appeared to necessitate a change in the people and their attitudes as a means to maintain momentum. This was achieved through the award of grants for staff development and through a change in hiring practices aimed at bringing in new faculty. Yet the informal culture at Middle State appeared to result in numerous activities throughout the campus that fell under the concept of visible actions. This differed from most developmental campuses, where centralized staff development is a key feature. Activities ranged from a faculty group that wrote one of the guiding documents that added new language to the campus lexicon to centrally administered developmental grants to a regular newspaper column that described efforts to incorporate technology into classrooms. All these efforts helped to build momentum throughout this informal environment.

Middle State created a local, departmental model faculty development program regarding technology. Leaders within different schools or colleges led the efforts to develop the needed support for their colleagues. The training programs were focused on the individuals and their needs. Bergquist's developmental culture would have predicted staff development as the most important strategy for change at Middle State. Yet that was not emphasized heavily on this campus. The culture of this unique campus also seemed to affect the way staff development was enacted. The informal and trusting nature of Middle State appeared to shape the staff development initiative, which was much more unstructured than on any of the other campuses in the entire project. This institution drew exclusively on internal staff for development because of the deep trust they held, knowing they would be the best guides for assisting each other's growth.

The two key strategies at Middle State were staff development and taking visible actions, clearly a reflection of the developmental culture. Less important within their change process were senior administrative support, vision, and collaborative leadership. The culture of the institution resulted in senior leadership being in the background of the change process. Furthermore, collaborative leadership was already the norm for the campus. Although a part of the change process, organizing activities and events for leaders across the campus to come together was not important within this informal, trusting environment. A flexible and opportunistic vision was important, but less so than staff development.

SUNSHINE COMMUNITY COLLEGE: MANAGERIAL, RESPONSIBLE, AND SELF-REFLECTIVE CULTURE

Within Bergquist's framework, the culture at Sunshine Community College is best classified as managerial. It is characterized by strong senior administrative directive, driven by goals, plans, and assessment; it is cognizant of outside forces pressing the institution and strives to meet customer needs; and it frequently experiences clashes in values between faculty and administrators.

Nonetheless, this campus differs from the managerial archetype in many ways. Sunshine has a strong commitment to student learning that transcends this large and complex four-campus college, which is why we label it *responsible*. Sunshine's responsible culture is not simply driven by managerial accountability but by a deeply human desire to help. Sunshine also is strongly *self-reflective*. Central administrators encourage introspection by the types of questions they continually ask faculty and campus administrators, as well as themselves. Faculty and administrators also spend significant time discussing "the way we do things around here" and how to improve those practices. Institutional leaders note that the environment is changing and seek to effect change on campus to align it with these external shifts. Information and data were collected not only to assess college goals but to understand institutional identity. There is a strong desire across the campus to understand Sunshine students and their needs and also to understand what Sunshine Community College is and how it works. Staff development, through workshops such as managing personal transformations (based on personal introspection), provides additional self-reflective mechanisms.

The Five Core Change Strategies and Sunshine's Culture

At the managerially oriented college, the senior administration provided very visible project leadership: developing the plan and a conceptual model to drive campus transformation, coordinating the leadership team, facilitating and coordinating communication among the four campuses, and securing external resources and reallocating internal ones. Sunshine also created a new position, vice president for transformation, to facilitate the campus' efforts.

At Sunshine, where the managerial culture had not historically created mechanisms for collaborative leadership, cross-campus input was a foreign concept. To tap leadership across the college, central administrators established several different committees. One of the first big steps in sharing leadership was to help people understand that they could now shape institutional direction and that their leadership was welcome. To promote shared leadership and to capture the good ideas from the faculty and staff, the institution held twelve college-wide forums and campus-structured dialogues. To demonstrate their willingness to share leadership, central administrators started writing "DRAFT" on all documents and encouraged written and electronic comments throughout the change process.

But collaborative leadership was unique compared with many other managerial cultures. Within most managerial cultures, the level of participation that Sunshine obtained at its dialogues, forums, and voluntary action teams would be atypical. The reason so many people attended the meetings was their commitment to students. This sense of responsibility led them to attend meetings where they were not sure if they would be heard, events that might simply be a waste of time. Also, Sunshine's focus on self-reflection seemed to make communication a core strategy; the forums and dialogues took on a distinctive form with people expressing feelings, beliefs, and interpretations. Collaboration on this campus meant that people needed to understand each other and themselves.

Flexible vision also played itself out uniquely at Sunshine. The leaders, working within the familiar managerial culture, gravitated toward having a mandated vision and clear plan. At first, they had difficulty creating a strategy that needed the requisite flexibility. After a slow start that included a rigid plan, the change leaders developed mechanisms by which they could design a process that was more opportunistic and flexible and yet stay focused. The message behind labeling every document with the word "DRAFT" symbolized the new approach. The leadership team also incorporated the comments from the various campus dialogues and feedback sessions in ways that continued to leave future options open. Outside pressures, in particular concerning performance indicators, also helped to promote the flexible yet focused design.

Yet there were ways that the flexible vision differed from what one might expect in other managerial cultures. For example, Sunshine attempted to develop a flexible vision through a series of data collection efforts. Data collection seemed to be such a strong element of vision because it reflected the campus's drive to be responsible and to become more self-aware. Some of the data collection mechanisms were extremely self-analytical, including an organizational character index and a collective vision index. These different assessments focused on learning about the nature of the organization and working to develop a more helpful culture and vision. Data collection focused on students was also seen as an important way to better respond to students' needs and to improve the learning environment.

Visible action was highly consistent with what one would expect in the managerial culture. At Sunshine, goals needed to be met to maintain the momentum for change. A short-term action team was established. This strategy created a surge of energy, bringing many holdouts to the change initiative.

At Sunshine, the decision to create the formal staff development program emerged from the president and vice president for transformation's office. Senior staff generated the list of program topics from the conversations they heard in the roundtables and through conversations with various faculty. The focus of the learning was how to develop staff to better serve the college, an objective that is closely aligned with a managerial culture rather than personal development for the individual, as was stressed at Middle State within its developmental culture. At Sunshine, staff development was an essential strategy in the change process, which appears to be related to their unique culture of self-reflection. This fact also runs counter to Bergquist's archetypal managerial culture, where flexible vision and senior administrative support are predicted to be the most important of the core strategies within it. It appears that Sunshine's great interest in self-reflection and personal transformation made staff development a high priority and successful strategy there.

METROPOLITAN UNIVERSITY: COLLEGIAL, AUTONOMOUS, AND INSECURE CULTURE

Metropolitan University reflects Bergquist's collegial culture. Colleges and schools are highly independent, and the institution is focused on research and the disciplines. One of Metropolitan's primary, if implicit, goals is to move up in the traditional academic rankings. Academic affairs issues and priorities dominate governance, and decision making occurs at the department and school levels.

Through the Tierney lens, the autonomous nature of Metropolitan far exceeds that described within the collegial archetype. The change initiative itself—to overhaul the curriculum, its structure, purposes, and pedagogies—results from a history of high fragmentation across the extremely autonomous schools and colleges and from an unfavorable accreditation review. The institution is private, which may contribute to the high level of autonomy—it is neither part of a system nor dependent on state funds, and it is responsible for its own resources in a continually shrinking fiscal environment. Central administrators in the past have had a high turnover rate, leaving colleges and schools responsible for their own continuity of purposes and for providing their own direction. Many people in the highly academic city in which the university is located view it as a low-status institution. New faculty are quickly socialized to learn that they work at a less-prestigious institution. Metropolitan has recently gone through a downturn in enrollment, creating significant financial distress at the university, which included laying off academic staff. Its insecurity was reinforced and heightened by the poor accreditation review.

The Five Core Change Strategies and Metropolitan's Culture

At collegial Metropolitan University, the provost and his administrative staff initially led the effort; they created a process that moved much of the key decision making to the faculty of each college. Senior administrative support took the role of launching the efforts and then providing resources and creating accountability mechanisms. Once the direction and goals were set, senior leaders were fairly absent from shaping decisions within each college and worked to intentionally stay out of the way. All decisions were pushed down to the college. The insecure and autonomous culture of Metropolitan seemed linked to the reliance on incentives as a major strategy for change. It appeared that incentives became the primary way that senior administrators could develop a sense of efficacy among their faculty and gain their commitment to a centralized change initiative.

Metropolitan reflected the collegial culture in its approach to collaborative leadership by tapping its decentralized administrative structure. Deans and chairs were expected to take leadership within their various units. The senior administrators delegated leadership to them and encouraged them to get faculty involvement and ownership in key unit decisions. Many valuable solutions to institutional problems were developed in cross-functional task forces that brought together faculty and staff from different units. Metropolitan also learned that it needed to place the word "DRAFT" on documents until there was official approval from each college. On a few occasions, a document was sent out without one or two schools' official approval, which led to disruption.

Another helpful insight through the Tierney framework is the way in which Metropolitan's autonomous culture related to collaborative leadership. Few institutions would "truly" delegate responsibility solely to the colleges and schools for the change initiative. But at Metropolitan, this was the only way to successfully achieve faculty ownership and buy-in. Many other initiatives had failed because leaders had not been attuned to this aspect of the culture on Metropolitan's campus. Several faculty noted that this respect for the nature of collaborative leadership is what made this particular initiative succeed.

Metropolitan's collegial culture was also evident in its strategies to create a flexible vision. Members of the campus immediately rejected the initial plan developed by the president as too restrictive and unwarranted. The responsibility for designing and implementing the change then shifted to the college and school levels. For example, the central administrators created a master document tracking aspects of the plan that had been delegated to the colleges and departments, yet central administrators allowed each unit to create the specifics to meet institutional goals. Careful communication, always in writing, existed between the various levels of the organization related to the vision and the change process. Central administrators also moderated the pace of change based on faculty feedback about the implementation scheduling.

The Tierney cultural framework also shed light on the flexible vision at Metropolitan. The central administration used campus insecurity as a lever to gain a commitment to their broad goals and strategies for change. They intentionally created a communications plan to gain commitment within the colleges and generate momentum. They widely publicized the good work of faculty and the success in the three pilot colleges. Past attempts to change were thwarted at Metropolitan because leaders could not coalesce the independent colleges. This time they found ways to build on faculty uneasiness over the curriculum and the unfavorable accreditation review. No generalized cultural archetypes would have been helpful in discovering these nuanced aspects of developing a robust design.

Taking visible action also followed the pattern expected at collegial culture. Metropolitan focused on resources as a motivation for change. The acquisition of several grants provided the needed incentive to advance the change initiative. Although each institution obtained grants for their initiatives, they seemed to be valued most at Metropolitan. Allocating grant money to faculty within departments at Metropolitan developed a sense of ownership and enthusiasm. The insecure culture at this campus seemed to use outside recognition, such as grant money and publicity, as a validation of its efforts. Although the collegial culture would have predicted that money would be important to taking action, the strong reliance on this strategy was not anticipated.

In Metropolitan's collegial culture, several different staff development models emerged. Many faculty were sent off campus to observe how their peers were working to transform general education. In addition, leaders brought to campus speakers who described new approaches to general education in particular disciplines, such as engineering. Experts within each college were also called on to describe innovative ideas and ways to facilitate the change process. The focus of many professional development efforts was at the departmental level; the outcome was that the faculty member could more effectively meet local objectives, which were in concert with the broad goals of general education.

The distinct culture at Metropolitan can also be seen in the way staff development emerged. The autonomy of Metropolitan appeared to have resulted in multiple levels of staff development by various colleges and schools and throughout levels within the college—department, program, and other levels. Its insecure culture seemed to make the institution seek outside expertise, not trusting its own knowledge for various aspects of the staff development.

In sum, the most important elements of change at Metropolitan were acquiring grants and incentives (taking visible actions), collaborative leadership, and vision. The collegial culture at Metropolitan focused on resources—both external grants and internal monetary rewards—as a marker of success, like many campuses with strong faculty and disciplinary values. The acquisition of several grants provided the needed incentive to legitimate the change initiative. The prestige of outside grants became the primary way that senior administrators could develop a sense of efficacy among insecure faculty. As would be predicted from their institutional culture, senior administrative support and staff development were less important within this culture.

INSIGHTS ABOUT INSTITUTIONAL CULTURE AND CHANGE

The emptiness of frequently offered generic advice, such as "leaders should support change," becomes clear through the previous examples.

Realizing that senior administrative support can take on a very different character based on distinctive institutional cultures is an important insight for change leaders. Simply following the lead of another institution without translating effective strategies into one's own culture may create more problems than solutions. Differences in the ways the strategies played themselves out within each culture reflect the importance of being aware of the institutional culture within which one operates.

The examples in this chapter show that each campus enacted a common set of strategies in different ways that were consistent with their own cultures. The distinctions are important: the approach to senior administrative support taken at Sunshine Community College most likely would not have been acceptable on the two other campuses, and vice versa. Ignoring institutional culture can thwart change processes. Where strategies for change violate cultural norms, change most likely will not occur (Eckel, 1998; Schein, 1992). The three case studies illustrate the shortsightedness of adopting change strategies "out of the box" and of the challenge to presenting change strategies as universal principles.

When institutions violated their institutional culture during the change process, they experienced difficulty. The process at Metropolitan, with its collegial nature, was almost halted when the senior administrators tried to lead the change directly. Not writing "DRAFT" on documents initially impeded the process at Sunshine, which was lacking awareness about the split between faculty and administrators within a managerial culture. Missteps in the change process are often a result of cultural misunderstandings. Leaders will likely be more successful in facilitating change if they take the time to truly understand the implicit as well as explicit elements of the cultures in which they are working.

A deeper understanding of institutional cultural may help change leaders determine which strategies might take prominence in the change process. For example, at Sunshine, staff development appeared to be the most important core strategy based on the self-reflective culture of the campus. At Middle State, collaborative leadership seemed to play a prominent role based on the family atmosphere on the campus. Also, certain substrategies emerged to play more prominent roles based on the culture of the institution, as incentives did at Metropolitan and communication at Sunshine. Understanding the strengths and relative contributions of different strategies may help leaders determine where best to focus efforts.

A final insight about how institutional culture and change are related is that Bergquist's four cultural archetypes can provide a helpful lens for understanding the ways in which culture is related to the change process.

There was a relationship between institutional cultural archetypes and the way the change process was enacted. For example, Metropolitan, a collegial campus, followed the predicted pattern of engaging in a change process in which faculty and traditional academic governance structures were central to the change process, motivation was derived from prestige, collaborative leadership used the traditional academic leaders, and key planning and decision making occurred at the college and departmental level. However, each campus's change process could not be explained through the archetypes alone. The self-reflective tendency of Sunshine would have been missed if only examined through Bergquist's managerial lens. A structured change process, as predicted by the developmental culture, most likely would have derailed the change effort at Middle State. And the lack of structure to support change at Middle State could not have been predicted by the developmental culture. Examining institutional culture in-depth, beyond the four archetypes, provides a deeper and richer understanding of the change process and appears to facilitate change.

CONCLUSION

These campus experiences have important implications for campus change agents. First, change agents should attempt to become cultural outsiders, or as Heifetz (1994) suggests, they need to be able to "get on the balcony" to see the patterns on the dance floor below. Reading institutional culture in order to develop and match the strategies for change is fundamental to an effective change process. Strategies used on these campuses for achieving this outside perspective included working with a network of institutions, using outside consultants, presenting at and attending conferences where they publicly explored their assumptions, bringing in new leadership, and asking new faculty hires to participate. Second, individuals or campuses interested in change may want to use Bergquist's typology or Tierney's framework to begin to understand better their culture and how it might effect transformational change processes.

Transformational change itself aims to alter culture in deep and pervasive ways; therefore, leaders should not be surprised that they need to be aware of culture in the way it affects the process of achieving that change. Leaders should become cultural analysts to assess and understand the cultures in which they are so entrenched, and they then need to become interpreters to translate these understandings to the ways they go about transformational change.

NOTE

1. This chapter is adapted with permission from Kezar, A., & Eckel, P. D. The effects of institutional culture on change strategies in higher education: Universal principles or culturally responsive concepts? *Journal of Higher Education, 73,* No. 4 (July/August 2002). Copyright 2002 by The Ohio State University Press. All rights reserved.

CHAPTER 7

The Mobile Model
of Transformation

O ver the course of this book, we have explored the idea of transformational change and compared it to other types of change,
described five core strategies essential for transformation and presented fifteen supporting strategies, discussed the importance of helping
people think differently and the role of culture, and illustrated the inter-
connections between the strategies. We have introduced the concept of
balance and shown the ways in which institutional culture shapes the
transformation process. We have covered a lot of ground. To make sense
of it all, this chapter places the components into a single model, which
we have named the Mobile Model. This model captures the complexity
of the transformation process and demonstrates the ways in which all of
the parts fit together. We use this chapter to present the model as a whole
and illustrate the ways in which it operated at two of the six transforming
institutions.

THE MOBILE MODEL

We create a descriptive metaphor to bring together and illustrate the
interworkings of the various components of transformation discussed
throughout this book together—the Mobile Model (see figure 7.1). Why
did we choose a mobile? We discovered that the change process, like a
mobile, is made up of various interdependent components (or strategies),
which, although they may move somewhat independently, are ultimately
connected directly or indirectly to one another. Mobiles, much like the

Figure 7.1
The Mobile Model for Transformational Change

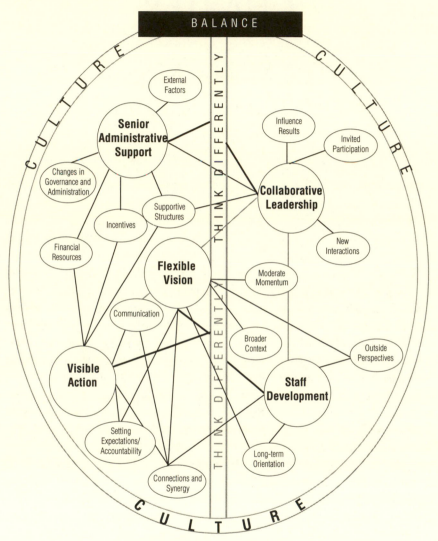

transformation process, require balance. Only as a whole is the mobile
functional; tipping any one part can upset the dynamic. A mobile also
swirls in the air currents, reflecting the constantly changing environment.
Much like institutional culture, in which each institution is unique and
yet as a group, the institutions reflect some common academic characteristics, the particular elements of a mobile may vary, and yet all mobiles
retain some common elements and abide by a defined set of principles.

The elements of a mobile are connected by something like a string. We compare these connections to the generation of new understandings. We found that what holds together the transformation process is the collective making of meaning. Finally, mobiles are affected by changing patterns of wind. Institutions that are undergoing transformation also are affected by shifts in their outside environments, which may alter some elements but rarely affect its core processes. We played with other descriptions, such as computers, brains, and organisms (Morgan, 1986), as well as communities, but they did not capture the complexities and interactions of the various elements or the importance of balance as did the mobile.

Our intent is to provide a comprehensive and coherent framework for change that leaders will find useful. We illustrate the components of the mobile model through two longer case studies: the experiences of Sunshine Community College and Metropolitan University. In the following section, we describe the transformation agendas and approaches to transformation for each institution. We then highlight the elements of the mobile model.

Sunshine Community College

Sunshine's initiative focused on moving the community college from an institution focused on teaching to one focused on learning. Sunshine is a much different campus from five years ago. The college has developed new academic support structures to facilitate learning. It has developed new faculty orientation and professional development programs to support learning. It has identified a set of widely agreed upon core competencies that shape academic program development and curricular revision. Faculty evaluation is now tied to illustrating evidence of learning through assessment rather than just focused on showing evidence of the teaching process. Retention rates have increased 20 percent, surpassing the college's initial retention goal, and student survey feedback suggests this increase is related to the intensified focus on learning. The importance of learning appears in all key campus documents, and it shaped the presidential search process. For the most part, faculty, staff, and administrators no longer think of teaching as the college's primary activity but instead focus on learning. The topics of conversations have changed to focus on learning, as have certain behaviors of faculty and administrators. The college has realigned its budget to support learning initiatives and has developed new opportunities for groups of faculty to work together to better understand principles of learning and develop courses and pedagogies that reflect their insights. The campus now proudly calls itself a learning-centered community college and has widespread cultural evidence to support that claim.

Sunshine formulated its transformation agenda after long discussions generated from the restlessness of top administrators and faculty leaders and an emerging belief that "students just weren't getting where we wanted them to get." In addition, close to 90 percent of new students required remediation. One administrator noted that "a lot of students were being lost who we felt didn't have to be lost if we could just focus more directly on learning and how people learn." At the same time, the state began the use of performance indicators, which created an additional external impetus to change and brought the need for assessing student learning into sharper focus.

Sunshine is a four-campus college serving fifty-four thousand students. Communication across geographic distances and departments and between faculty, administrators, and community stakeholders was difficult. Developing a shared understanding of key issues and priorities was tenuous, and a coordinated effort to effect change was trying. The institution began its change effort by establishing a planning team of faculty leaders and senior administrators, charging it with developing a process for buy-in and communication. This group hired external consultants from business and education and read the change literature to inform the process they were going to develop. In their final report, the leaders noted that these activities "allowed the team to take on the role of students by learning more about their own institution, listening to outside impartial experts, and listening and learning from each other." After developing a common language through reading and interacting with the outside consultants, the leadership team crafted a unifying change agenda that brought together a number of change efforts presently underway at the college. Some of these efforts were isolated to a single department or campus within the system. Others were college-wide. "One of our key tasks was to step back and take a look at the larger picture and the way in which they could leverage change by tying efforts together," wrote the team in one of its reports.

The leadership team of vice presidents and faculty leaders developed an initial three-year plan, which was revisited, expanded, and extended over the course of the work. The activities included holding structured dialogues, developing consensus on a college-wide vision, gathering baseline data and assessing core processes, understanding organizational culture, forming teams to work on specific issues and to identify cross-institutional activities, training faculty and staff and developing their

leadership skills (added later by campus leaders), designing and implementing improved communications and decision-making processes (added
later by campus leaders), and designing mechanisms to evaluate progress.
The team started with a rationalistic, managerial, and structural emphasis,
as evidenced by the leaders' emphasis on visioning and developing evaluation mechanisms. Over time, they adopted a more developmental and
values-oriented approach. For instance, the change leaders noted that
they learned the importance of faculty and staff development and the
importance of reinforcing central ideas in speeches and various events
related to the new initiative, as well as the importance of reinforcing
values through discussion and dialogue. Their plans and strategies evolved
as the leadership team sought feedback throughout the process, something
else they learned was important throughout the change process.

As a central approach to their change efforts, the leadership team organized sets of campuswide roundtables. The first set was twelve roundtable conversations. Every faculty and staff member received an invitation
to the roundtables. Approximately three hundred faculty and staff, including nearly every full-time faculty member, attended one of the roundtables. These conversations focused on what it would mean for Sunshine
to be a learning-centered community college and to make recommendations for changes that would accomplish that vision. Leadership team
members facilitated the roundtables where they described the external
forces affecting the campus and why change was necessary. Comments
from the roundtables were compiled and circulated college-wide, and all
faculty and staff were invited to comment. New insights were incorporated into a document reflecting the conversations and circulated college-
wide. Based on the rounds of discussions, the leadership team developed
a draft definition of a learning-centered community college. They decided
to keep the statement as a perpetual draft, to be revised as collective
thinking evolved. Later in the process, the leadership team initiated a
second set of roundtable conversations. This time involving close to 170
people, these conversations resulted in the creation of four action teams.
A third set of roundtable conversations occurred at a fall welcome back
retreat to respond to the work of the action teams.

Senior administrators gave strong support. For example, two vice presidents led the campus team charged with managing the change process.
The president constantly articulated the importance of the change initiative and took a lead role in writing to all the members of the college
community about the change project. He also facilitated some of the
roundtables, was an active participant in the leadership team meetings,

and provided financial resources. One faculty member noted: "Without the resources and commitment of the senior administration, from the president down, things would be the same as they had always been." In addition, the president provided resources for one key recommendation from the roundtables—to create a new position, vice president for institutional transformation, to provide resources and focus for the change initiative.

Campus leaders realized early in the process the importance of validating the good things already occurring. Many faculty and administrators believed they were already doing things well, and recognizing this fact made people feel worthwhile during the change process. The president noted:

We have learned that educators will fear change less if we focus first on what we want to preserve. We should not throw out the baby with the bath water and abandon the higher calling that we, as educators, share. By articulating our core values and our core purposes, as well as acknowledging that these are enduring aspects of the college, change becomes less frightening since it represents an effort to better serve that which we hold most dear.

This realization led to the development of a "vision and organizational character action team." With the assumption that any significant change at the college should be rooted in commonly held core values, the team administered an organizational character index to determine perceptions of the institution's character. As part of this process, people in various units throughout the campus filled out a detailed survey instrument. The leaders believed that transformation would require different types of support and leadership depending on how the college perceives itself. Sunshine used this information to design appropriate change strategies and thereby improve the prospect for success.

Following the first set of roundtables, change leaders held a two-and-a-half-day Transformation Workshop with 170 persons attending to create a common understanding of change, review the findings of the twelve roundtables, widen the circle of involvement, and make recommendations about how best to move forward. Following the workshop, a call for volunteers was sent college-wide, and over 180 persons volunteered to serve on a set of four "action teams." The leadership team also created several other opportunities for involvement. As one faculty member noted: "It is no longer a surprise to be asked to participate in a collaborative effort. Making people feel part of the process is important. Another thing we did right was sharing articles and discussing; this helps prepare people for possible future involvement."

A symbolic step to improve involvement was to use the word *draft* frequently, not only on the college's vision statement but also on all documents associated with transformation. One administrator said, "We learned to put the word DRAFT in big letters at the top of everything. If you don't do anything else, do that. People don't want to think it's over and done with before they've had a chance to be heard."

From the intensified conversations and widespread involvement, those leading the change efforts and others involved realized that different subgroups viewed the campus and its work differently. Leaders realized that until people began to appreciate these differences, progress would be stalled. Leaders intentionally surfaced troubled relationships; issues of lack of trust and conflicts in priorities were openly discussed. They provided forums for faculty and administrators to discuss the perceptions they held of each other and to work through their difference. Faculty in vocational and liberal arts areas examined points of contentiousness. These cross-unit dialogues revealed basic assumptions and deeply held philosophies. They resulted in difficult but eventually useful clarifying debates about common purposes, particularly on difficult questions such as, "Why should we serve business and industry if the college is a learning institution?"

At this point, people noticed that the institution was engaged in a lot of talk that was, in their belief, generating little action. One administrator commented:

After about a year of reflection, roundtables and opportunities to talk about what a learning-centered institution would look like, we were still talking. And one of the things we learned then very rapidly was that we needed to make a way for action to take place. So we formed a short-term action team. And those people who were ready to roll and wanted to do "something-anything-now" were invited to participate in that. We did find that there were a number of suggestions that came out of our many roundtables that didn't require six years to accomplish and gave people a sense that something was happening. Make sure that you give some means for some kind of short-term action so that people can see some progress.

One short-term outcome was a 20 percent increase in graduation/completion rates. This provided an important indicator of the institution's commitment and focus on students and helped generate substantial momentum.

Sunshine was poised to act, having taken the time to develop a common understanding and vision of what being learning centered would mean for that particular community college. An important step was developing a leadership institute, a coordinated effort that provides ongoing professional development opportunities for all employees. The content was shaped by the work of the action teams and by the roundtables. After the first three years more than 1,237 faculty and staff participated in the 123 courses and workshops offered. The college purchased and renovated a house into a small conference facility used exclusively for the leadership courses. One specific set of workshops focused on personal and organizational change. One set of activities was the Discipline Enrichment Series, which brought together faculty teaching in similar departments to discuss issues related to teaching and learning. This was the first time these conversations had occurred across the college's four campuses. It helped faculty teaching in the same fields but at different campuses to collaboratively enhance learning in that discipline.

Finally, campus leaders learned not to assume automatic buy-in and trust but to realize that these ideas need to be continually reinforced. As one member of the leadership team put it, "We really had to learn the hard way that no one was trying to push anything on anyone. There was no hidden agenda. That is something we have to continually work at." Campus leaders learned that continual openness and working to help people to be part of the change process were critical and that change just takes longer for some people.

Metropolitan University

Metropolitan University, a private, urban research university, is revising its curriculum to achieve the learning objectives common to general education through the major. The initiative's goal is to provide students with a more coherent education. Through this initiative, known as the Common Academic Charter (CAC), faculty across the various colleges are crafting general education outcomes that are connected to all curricular components, such as liberal arts courses, disciplinary courses, and non-course experiences modules. Metropolitan has met several of its goals, including a new curriculum, evidence of greater coherence through student and faculty evaluation, and involvement of more than 75 percent of the faculty. Students and faculty no longer perceive their general education courses as a "mishmash" of unrelated experiences. Faculty and administrators describe learning objectives, rather than content areas, as the focus of the undergraduate experience. Behavioral changes include experiential learning opportunities, regular working groups across schools and departments, ongoing communication across units, and enhanced student outcomes. Some of the main sustainability mechanisms include a newsletter, new faculty-led committees, and a speaker's series on student learning and the general education.

The pressure for change came internally, from faculty and administrators who recognized that the current structure of general education was simply not working, and externally from an accreditation review that cited the institution for its lack of common educational experiences. The fragmentation in the curriculum was not surprising to campus administrators as it reflected the high degree of independence of Metro's colleges and departments. The institution describes itself as a series of loosely connected colleges that prided themselves on their autonomy. It was rare for anyone beyond top administrative leaders to take responsibility for the institution as a whole. Because of the decentralized nature of the institution, the president and provost intentionally created processes that were consistent with the decentralized character of the institution and with faculty leaders, who were more concerned about the direction and activities of their own individual colleges. An earlier attempt to create a university-wide core curriculum failed in part because, according to some, the professional programs resisted adding new required courses to already highly structured curricula.

At the same time as it received the poor accreditation report highlighting the curricular problem, the institution faced a 30 percent drop in enrollment that, in turn, created financial hard times for the tuition-driven institution. In addition, the institution recently had been reclassified from a Doctoral II to a Research II institution, jumping two categories in the former Carnegie classification system. As one person described the impact: "While research and teaching is not an either/or proposition, the desire for upward mobility in the research world often finds institutions sending conflicting messages about its core values." These were the challenges facing a new president and provost.

The central administration, primarily the provost, was instrumental, crafting a process to implement the CAC based on the premise that the campus community had to identify its own educational goals. This view was key to gaining support for an initiative that was an extreme departure from the traditional general education curricula. The administration formed an institution-wide committee of faculty, administrators, and students to develop a common set of undergraduate experiences regardless of discipline. This task force developed a newsletter to convey its ideas and continuously sought feedback and input from the campus over the course of their efforts. Identifying common goals took eighteen months, from October 1992 to June 1994. The second component of the change process, which ran concurrently with the first, was to design the implementation mechanism. Campus leaders identified their challenge as to "devise a mechanism for general education that respected the university's culture." A central principle was campus involvement, not only in developing the shared goals but also in designing their implementation mechanism.

Once the goals and the processes were developed, the administrators moved to gain the approval of Metropolitan's various governing bodies. The CAC gained approval from the faculty senate, the faculty in full, and the board of trustees when it became a component of the institution's strategic plan. The newsletters and forums held earlier also served as means for gaining early legitimacy for the initiative. The Deans' Council and the Undergraduate Curriculum Committee unanimously approved it. Even the student government, on its own initiative, passed a resolution supporting the newly articulated goals. At this point, administrators believed they finally were ready to begin implementation. Metropolitan's provost and vice provost decided to use pilot projects in three volunteer colleges: Business and Management, Allied Health, and Nursing. Next, administrators worked to implement the CAC across the remaining colleges. Senior administrators designed an implementation strategy with three simultaneous phases. Each college was asked to (1) conduct an audit to determine the extent to which the identified CAC goals were already being met, (2) develop a detailed implementation plan that would result in "a redefinition of the curricula in light of the shared educational goals," and (3) develop a process of periodic assessment, for which some colleges tapped accrediting bodies. Although each college moved forward through its own process, the common goals of the CAC helped constrain Metropolitan's fragmentation while respecting the institution's culture of college autonomy.

To develop collaboration across units, institutional leaders "encouraged horizontal, interdisciplinary involvement around shared goals" and created cross-unit interest groups working on challenges such as writing competency within disciplines, information literacy, and experiential education, and around topics such as esthetics, the natural world, and ethics. These interest groups sponsored annual workshops. The leader of each interest group received a small stipend to acknowledge the extra work. In addition to the interest groups, the institution developed a series of workshops and activities to support the implementation. For example, by October 1995, more than 150 faculty from the colleges that served as pilots had participated in CAC workshops. Some additional activities to advance CAC objectives included department retreats and a series of symposia featuring nationally prominent speakers on topics such as the future of undergraduate education, critical thinking, and technology in the classroom. In addition, faculty were encouraged to attend related off-campus conferences. The interest groups and workshops allowed faculty from different units to discuss topics related to the CAC and have conversations about institutional goals and the processes. In one report, administrators wrote:

For the CAC to be successful, faculty within each unit must talk with each other about the curriculum. Some chairs and deans have used the implementation of CAC as a mechanism for beginning to talk about unit goals. As implementation has progressed, the CAC is being seen as part of a broader university-wide change to a more student-centered institution. This has been important because there are numerous initiatives underway at the university. To the extent that they are connected, the burden on faculty and administrators is less.

As part of their implementation process, senior administrative leaders developed an internal departmental grants competition, with the units receiving between $10,000 and $20,000 for their CAC initiatives. As was noted in one report, "This [award] was large enough for most departments to be a valuable incentive." In addition, the president, provost, and vice provost seized all possible opportunities to talk about CAC on- and off-campus, where they stressed the significance of the CAC to institutional goals. Administrators also brought in external resources that allowed the campus the needed flexibility at a time of tight budgets. They secured a $250,000 implementation grant from the Fund for the Improvement of Postsecondary Education (FIPSE), a $200,000 institution-wide reform grant from the National Science Foundation (NSF) for developments in math, science, engineering, and technology, and $150,000 from a private foundation to implement one of the pilot projects. In addition to outside money, they were able to get *Science* magazine to highlight their efforts. One report noted: "All these funds and the publicity, while not large, provided external validation of our change initiative; this was especially important to the researchers on campus. These funds combined with internally available funds have provided the seeds to encourage change in the various units." The provost also hired an administrator to oversee the CAC implementation. In addition, each of the colleges identified a CAC coordinator to lead implementation efforts for that college. The coordinators received a stipend and met periodically with each other and the campus CAC director to discuss common issues related to implementation.

Finally, those responsible for implementing the CAC across campus developed an "intentional on-campus publicity campaign." They developed a CAC newsletter that included drafts of documents, requests for input, bibliographies of related publications (which were also put on reserve in the library), examples of courses that adopted CAC goals, and announcements of workshops and funding opportunities related to CAC. Regarding the implementation plan, administrators wrote:

Introduction of CAC throughout the undergraduate programs has occurred slowly and unevenly. Some of that was deliberate; a widening group of faculty and administrators must buy into the process and the desired outcomes if we are to actually transform undergraduate education. Some units, particularly in the professional colleges, saw the CAC as an opportunity to better meet the goals that they and their accreditors have for student education and they forged ahead. Other units hoped that the ACE would go away. . . . Ideally, units will "own" this change; it will not be foisted on them. Thus, the balance between top-down pressure and bottom-up enthusiasm (or lack thereof) continues to be a strategic issue.

Core Strategies

The core strategies used at these two institutions are clearly visible. At Sunshine, *senior administrative support* resulted in financial resources for the initiative, incentives, several new structures to support the effort, the creation and support of an extensive faculty and staff development program, the articulation of philosophy that values what the campus currently does well that in turn made people feel appreciated, and changes in the decision-making processes. At Metropolitan, senior administrators, primarily the provost and associate provost, were responsible for launching the initiative and shepherding the early discussions that allowed the campus community to identify common educational goals. They sought outside funds at a time when the institution could not internally reallocate monies, and they created a competition for substantial resources ($10,000–$20,000).

The president and other senior staff at Sunshine actively fostered an atmosphere of *collaborative leadership*. The leadership team, which itself was composed of individuals from across the four colleges and both faculty and administrators, created avenues for involvement through workshops, symposia, and roundtables, with open invitations throughout the process. Faculty leaders shaped the processes used to engage the rest of campus and played important roles in facilitating the various roundtables and drafting key documents. All plans and ideas were drafts, encouraging people to participate and influence the outcomes and process.

At Metropolitan, the most telling illustration of collaborative leadership was the freedom central administrators gave to each unit to design their own curricular changes around agreed-upon goals. Rather than dictate a centralized implementation formula, central administrators allowed each college to develop its own audit process to determine the extent to which it already met CAC objectives, develop its own implementation process, and craft its own system of assessment. Leadership emerged in each college to bring about the needed changes. The cross-functional interest groups also illustrate collaborative leadership; they allowed interested faculty to share similar concerns and engage in collective problem solving on an agenda that they set.

Having a flexible plan with a clear sense of direction to move forward was a central element to guide institutional actions at both campuses. The *flexible vision* at Sunshine emerged out of several prior years of campuswide dialogue, which was refined by the leadership team (and outside consultants) and shared with the entire campus. The flexible vision helped to create an orientation—student learning—that the college collectively defined and embraced out of the culture of the institution and which reflected institutional values and beliefs. At Metropolitan, the flexible vision was based on the widely shared beliefs that the curriculum was not delivering everything it should and that the lack of common educational objectives was leading to a negative impact on the institution's ability to provide a top-quality educational experience. The vision, which focused on learning objectives, was drafted in a way that allowed each autonomous college to act in its own way, but that fell within an agreed-upon framework. Departments could see that the CAC would allow them to further pursue their own educational goals and to meet the objectives of their specialized accrediting bodies.

At Sunshine, *staff development* was critical to fostering new knowledge and skills related to being student centered as well as in developing collaborative leadership. The Leadership Academy helped provide people with the leadership skills to communicate more effectively, make decisions, and provide input on the change initiative. Staff development provided participants with information and language to help bring about the desired changes. Metropolitan provided numerous opportunities for faculty development. For example, the interest groups that explored specific topics related to implementing the CAC provided opportunities for faculty responsible for implementing the initiative to explore questions through engagement with colleagues and readings. Metropolitan also provided faculty development opportunities by bringing nationally prominent speakers to campus, by holding symposia and workshops, and by encouraging and supporting faculty to attend national conferences.

Visible action was essential for Sunshine to maintain momentum. The large numbers of people participating in the roundtables and at the Leadership Academy were important indicators that the campus was engaged in something serious and important. The documents that resulted from the roundtables and the work of the action teams, particularly the short-term action team, helped mark progress. At Metropolitan, much if not all of the real work associated with implementing the CAC was visible. In addition, faculty participated in widely recognized discussion groups and attended campuswide forums, newsletters detailed the work of various groups, and three colleges launched successful and highly visible pilot projects. The overwhelming support by various campus governance bodies was an important visible step toward progress.

Both of these institutions engaged in strategies beyond the five core ones discussed here. Change leaders at both institutions put their issues in a broader context. They set expectations for behavior and held people accountable along the way. They invited participation throughout the process, and in many different ways, and created new ways for groups to interact through roundtables, retreats, development opportunities, and cross-unit working groups, to identify a few activities. Those who participated could see their influence on the process and its outcomes. Leaders moderated progress and the pace of change; they knew when to push the campus to act and when to back off and set specific challenges for the campus or different units to address without overwhelming them. They created support structures and found financial resources needed to do new things. They modified their administrative and decision-making structures and made important connections and synergy between groups and components of the change process. They used outside groups wisely and tapped external perspectives to advance on-campus efforts. Finally, they developed extensive communication strategies that used multiple outlets, some long-standing and others created specifically for the transformation work.

Interrelationship of Strategies, Nonlinear Process, and Balance

These two cases also show the important relationships between the core and secondary change strategies. Strategies were bundled together, and some occurred simultaneously. The familiar progression of discrete steps suggested by most traditional change models did not occur. For example, taking action helped to build collaborative leadership at Sunshine, whereas senior administrative support facilitated collaborative leadership at Metropolitan. Realizing that strategies are interconnected and nonlinear helped institutions advance their efforts. Some additional examples illustrate this point.

At Sunshine, connected to flexible vision were secondary strategies such as obtaining and incorporating outside perspectives, working within the institutional culture, creating synergy and connections, putting change into a broader context, taking a long-term orientation, influencing the results, and communicating effectively. Leaders appeared to be successful because they intentionally referred to external factors, which allowed campus members to understand better the rationale driving change by putting the initiative into a broader context. The planning team made a concerted effort to communicate these outside perspectives to people within the institution as part of developing the flexible vision through the roundtables. In addition, the vision was not first developed and then communicated. Instead, the roundtables shaped the plan's development, allowing individuals to influence the outcomes.

At Metropolitan, senior administrative support was linked to developing support structures, providing financial resources, creating incentives, and using external factors constructively. External factors, such as the involvement of associations and foundations, played important roles throughout the process. Senior administrative leaders helped create new structures, such as faculty development programs, and facilitated new types of interactions through the cross-functional team. These were important strategies to effect change and not simply outcomes of change processes, as is suggested frequently in the change literature. Senior administrators secured new resources and created departmental incentives over the course of the change process to keep the campus focused on the challenges ahead and to support the work being done in the various colleges.

Balance was also important among various change strategies and to the process itself. Leaders at Sunshine balanced inside and outside perspectives. They found a balance between long- and short-term goals and tasks by creating a long-term plan and coupling this with short-term action teams. They also created a balance between historic priorities and new initiatives. Finally, they balanced senior administrative leadership with a collaborative process.

At Metropolitan, leaders struck a balance between a quick pace of change and the need for buy-in and involvement, which took more time. Administrators spoke about the importance of moderating the pace of change, as they needed to bring people along and spend time engaging in activities that help people think differently. They also balanced inside and outside perspectives and expertise. The change efforts also balanced centrally initiated tasks and activities with those of the autonomous colleges. Rather than let each college work completely independently, change leaders created structures that were consistent with Metropolitan's culture of autonomy. Finally, the premise of the CAC initiative was based on a new balance of responsibilities between each college and the institution for the goals of the general education curriculum.

Thinking Differently

The core strategies, together with many of the supporting strategies, were effective as a package because, in addition to their individual instrumental contributions, they facilitated thinking differently. They provided institutions with multiple opportunities for key participants to create new understandings of the institution's direction and priorities, of their roles in the transforming institution, and of the ways that common notions, such as teaching, service, participation, are evolving and what they now mean. Thinking differently helps people collectively make sense out of uncertain and ambiguous or changing organizational situations and understand what the changes mean for them (March, 1994; Weick, 1995).

For example, the roundtables and cross-unit interest groups at Sunshine and Metropolitan provided opportunities for people to make new meaning from the proposed change and to begin to understand their individual places in the newly emerging realities. Both institutions capitalized on faculty and staff development opportunities for helping individuals to personalize the change and think about what it will mean in relation to their jobs, responsibilities, and identities. Both institutions brought external consultants and speakers to campus and developed workshops and symposia that provided opportunities to develop a collective understanding about the change agenda and process.

Part of meaning making at Sunshine was to recast the contentious relationships between faculty and administrators. Realizing that some faculty distrusted the change process and the administrators, and thought there was a hidden agenda, the leadership team carefully engaged those critics and allowed them to air their concerns in public forums. Every form of data collected—the institutional reports, document analysis, interviews, and site visits—helped to reinforce the new sense through the collective interpretation of data.

Culture

Culture affects the process and strategies used to bring about change. Important characteristics of Sunshine's culture were its customer focus and strong sense of accountability. These characteristics made the college open to external feedback and to data that facilitated change. They also helped to make assessment and evaluation easier to implement and central to the change process. Institutional culture made the choice to gather baseline data and to set up a team to evaluate the campus character palatable to the various key constituents. Sunshine's culture of accountability influenced the type of involvement that comprised collaborative leadership; people felt that an important role was to provide feedback that would hold leaders accountable to their public commitments. Finally, Sunshine's managerial culture allowed senior leaders to play major roles in designing and facilitating the change process.

The culture at Metropolitan was characterized first and foremost by the high autonomy of the colleges. For instance, the explanation for past failures at developing a common unifying curriculum was that the proposed ideas did not fit within some of the professional colleges, which strongly resisted centrally derived modifications to their curriculum. Second, most important decisions at the institution tended to be made at the college level. Leaders recognized that rather than a centralized effort with a representative committee making recommendations, the broad goals of CAC needed to be developed so that individual colleges could adapt them to fit their own goals and curricula. Local control and responsibility meant everything. Because of the autonomous culture, simply bringing together people from different units who shared common interests created tremendous energy and brought creativity to the effort. Finding common interest between diverse faculty was a new way of operating. These interest groups helped spark important conversations. Being aware of the culture helped leaders address issues within the culture that might hinder the change process.

Summary: Keys to the Model

Perhaps the most critical element of the Mobile Model is the relationship of helping people think differently to the transformational change process. This study suggests that large-scale institutional change is about meaning construction—or more exactly in times of change, reconstruction—a phenomenon known in the organizational behavior literature as organizational sensemaking (Gioia & Chittipeddi, 1991; March, 1994; Weick, 1995). Those institutions that made the most progress toward their change initiative had processes that facilitated new thinking and the creation of new understandings. The importance of thinking differently reinforces the findings of studies related to other organizational processes in which interpretation is seen as most essential to the work of colleges and universities (Birnbaum, 1991; Bolman & Deal, 1991; Chaffee, 1991). Various scholars, including Senge (1992) and Weick (1995), have suggested the importance of making new meaning and adaptive learning within organizations, but they have not explored this concept in relation to transformational change. Practitioners have been left on their own to determine how these concepts play themselves out in everyday organizational life as well as in times of major change. The experiences of institutions in this project provide clues for campus change agents to develop strategies that provide ample time to explore, discuss, and create new interpretations and meanings that shape activities and behaviors.

The five core strategies can guide leaders through the transformational change process, providing an alternative to the sometimes disparate and overwhelming change literature. This book provides leaders with not only a set of clear strategies but also a detailed understanding of how the strategies both play themselves out independently as well as work together to facilitate transformation. For example, the diverse experiences of the institutions in this study show that staff development can take many different forms from a series of workshops to a one-day forum to a semester-long seminar, can involve people from across campus or focus on a single department, and can have a formal or informal curriculum. These nuances about staff development and our discussion of institutional culture help to provide campus change agents with the necessary context-based knowledge to undertake staff development in ways that advance transformation on their own campuses.

Most studies of change and transformation pay little attention to the relationship of change strategies to one another. They frequently present change as a linear process; for instance, teleological models present change as a series of sequenced, planned events (Kezar, 2001). Institutions recognized the importance of moving ahead on a number of activities, in a number of areas, concurrently. Transformation was not a straight, linear process, but instead one that was comprised of activities and strategies that were interconnected and occurred simultaneously. The concept of balance, in particular, is strongly related to the success of executing multiple strategies.

CONCLUSION: PUTTING THE MODEL INTO PRACTICE

The Mobile Model provides a structure to conceptualize the transformation process. Therefore, we recommend campus leaders follow a few initial steps: (1) ask a set of key questions; (2) create a collaborative process, possibly through campus reading groups; (3) develop strategies for understanding campus culture; and (4) provide criteria and a process for charting transformation.

Campus leaders should initiate the process by beginning a dialogue about challenging questions. The first set of questions for leaders to ask themselves (and their institutions) is: Why do we need to change and how much change is needed? Are we seeking to undertake transformation or some other type of change? The experiences of project institutions suggest that the magnitude of change will help dictate the strategies used. In chapter 2, we described the characteristics of transformational change and compared it with other types of change. Something that separates transformational change from other types of change is its focus on institutional culture. Campuses need to ask themselves whether the proposed change will affect the values and basic assumptions of the campus. Another challenge is to map the effects of the proposed change because transformational change is deep and pervasive, affecting the entire institution. Mapping the effects of the proposed change and attempting to explore the ways in which various units and individuals might be affected were useful to determine the proposed change's depth and pervasiveness. It is easy to say that everything needs to change; it is another to map out the change and clearly examine the ways that various units would be required to modify their work in order to carry out the proposed change. Transformational change is also intentional. Because the campuses are embarking on transformational change, it seems apparent that the process is intentional. However, do other forces exist that are driving change to which the institution is simply reacting with little coordinated or examined effort? How can these pressures be linked to create a more intentional response? Finally, transformation requires a long-term effort and commitment. To what extent does the proposed change need to be sustained over time by people throughout the campus? What is the expected implementation period? How realistic is that timetable? Many of the transforming institutions in the project revised their anticipated timetable in light of newfound knowledge about transformation and their institutional culture. Others did not compromise their expected time frame and instead decided to seek less-ambitious change.

The Mobile Model stresses the idea that transformation requires a collaborative approach. Getting people to think differently, as essential to bringing about transformation, is a collaborative and collective process. An open and inclusive process is consistent with higher education's tradition of shared governance. Effective approaches for developing buy-in and building awareness campuswide will vary depending on the specific transformation agenda and, as we demonstrate, the institution's culture. However, one effective strategy that we saw used by a number of institutions is a campus reading group. Reading groups build on highly developed academic strengths such as inquiry, focused thought, writing, and contemplation to advance institutional goals. Reading groups and other similar processes focus collective attention, bring people together who otherwise might not interact, let alone problem solve, surface institutional assumptions, interpretations, and biases, and provide a common knowledge base from the readings explored.

The model also suggests that understanding one's institutional cultural is essential to transformation. However, simply being aware that institutional culture affects organizational processes may not be enough to make smart decisions about how best to proceed with transformational change. Instead, leaders need a deeper understanding of the specific history, traditions, and norms that will separate effective from ineffective strategies. For example, as we learned, involvement is not enough. It is the particular type of involvement that is consistent with expectations and norms that will determine if change proceeds or is derailed. Although understanding one's culture comprehensively can be difficult, tools and strategies exist to help, including outside consultants or bringing in individuals from other institutions. Institutions can also gain the "outsider" perspective through intentional self-discovery (Heifetz, 1994; Wheatley, 1994). Institutional change leaders can to ask themselves questions such as: To what degree are we a collegial, political, developmental, or managerial culture? The work of Bergquist (1992) and Tierney (1991) can be helpful. Kuh and Whitt (1988) also offer a process for conducting a cultural audit that can serve as a model including observation, interviewing key informants, focus groups, and document analysis. Cultural audits can help identify the basic assumptions held by various individuals and groups by which appropriate behavior in their institution is determined.

Third, as campus leaders work to understand the nuances of their cultures and how they may shape the change process, they should develop some baseline data for indicating or measuring transformation to show visible progress. Before engaging in the work of transformation, campus leaders might outline the structural and cultural indicators discussed in Chapter 2 as a template to mark progress, keeping in mind the importance of both long- and short-term goals. These benchmarks will help campus change leaders articulate where the institution is at and where it should go and are keys to providing visible progress important to transformational change. Baseline data and an assessment strategy to chart an institution's progress on its transformation agenda can also help leaders counter arguments by naysayers and make the case for why change is necessary to foundations and other outsiders that can be used to leverage future work. In sum, it should be clear from these first three steps that change leaders need to lay important groundwork for the transformation process; quickly jumping in and changing just to get something done might impede future progress.

Although we can provide broad directions about moving ahead with transformation, providing specific guidance is difficult because, as discussed throughout the book, there are many paths depending on an institution's current situation, its transformation agenda, its culture, and the environment. What will work for one institution, as the varied journeys of the six transforming institutions suggest, may not be efficacious for another institution. This is why we provide detailed descriptions throughout the book. For instance, at Sunshine, the first step was to set up a committee that would spend time developing an agenda. So they began with collaborative leadership. This approach differed markedly from Metropolitan, where the provost spent time outlining the process and then communicating it to others and, therefore, senior administrative support was enacted first. What characterized these two processes, as well as those at the other four transforming institutions, however, was that early in their transformation efforts, change leaders found ways to make a convincing case that change was needed. Their efforts jump-started the transformation process. It is important to note that to accomplish this, it was not the specific strategy but rather that leaders used a variety of activities to initiate transformation that was important.

As a closing thought, we want to remind readers that the process of transformation is difficult, complex, and messy. We learned that from where the leaders stood in the middle of this chaos, their efforts often looked like failures, even at institutions that we identify as transforming. Leaders could easily see the road ahead, but only with careful and conscious efforts could they look at the ground they had covered. Progress is difficult to notice when every day presents new challenges. The orderly approaches such as planning, business process reengineering, or traditional strategic change have often failed to facilitate change in higher education because of the complexity of the task and the operating characteristics of the institutions (Birnbaum, 2000). However, the complex journeys of the six transforming institutions discussed here show that transformation can occur and that it requires multiple strategies happening concurrently, strategies that change cultures while remaining consistent with those cultures and that generate new meanings and ways of thinking. This pill of complexity may be a hard one to swallow when so many management texts and much administrative common wisdom call for highly rational, straightforward process. But the interactivity, synergy, and overlapping elements of the Mobile Model will help to bring about necessary deep and pervasive changes that we call transformation.

APPENDIX

Institutions in the ACE Project on Leadership and Institutional Transformation

Ball State University (IN)
Bowie State University (MD)
California State Polytechnic University, Pomona
Centenary College of Louisiana
The City College of the City University of New York
College of DuPage (IL)
El Paso Community College District (TX)
Kent State University (OH)
Knox College (IL)
Maricopa County Community College District (AZ)
Michigan State University
Mills College (CA)
Northeastern University (MA)
Olivet College (MI)
Portland State University (OR)
Seton Hall University (NJ)
State University of New York College at Geneseo
Stephen F. Austin University (TX)
University of Arizona
University of Hartford (CT)
University of Massachusetts, Boston

University of Minnesota
University of Puerto Rico, Rio Piedras
University of Wisconsin-La Crosse
Valencia Community College (FL)
Wellesley College (MA)

APPENDIX

Research Design and Methodology

This appendix outlines the research design and methodology we used in this analysis of the ACE Project on Leadership and Institutional Transformation. It discusses case selection, data collection and analysis, and methodological rigor and limitations.

Two different schools of research related to organizational change exist: the content school and the process school. Researchers in the content school have focused on antecedents and consequences of change, typically utilizing large samples and statistical methods. In contrast, researchers in the process school have focused on the role of actors in the change process. This study falls into the second school, focusing on how the process of a particular type of change occurs. Researchers within this tradition tend to use case study and methodology within the qualitative tradition. Based on the process focus of the study and the lack of detailed data within higher education to study the process of change, we utilized a case study approach because our goal was to examine a host of different institutional types with varying change agendas. Detailed ethnographic studies are also needed; however, this methodology did not suit the goal of this study to understand institutional differences and to study a range of institution types. Case study methodology was identified as the best way to study a process across various institution types.

Understanding organizational change is a complicated, contextual, and confounding process that calls for a method that accounts for such elements (Pettigrew, 1995). Case studies are useful because they allow researchers to collect information from a variety of informants and materials across the organization, helping to form a complicated picture that allows for diverse and often competing explanations of the phenomenon for a deeper understanding (Stake, 1995). This method is most appropriate when three conditions are present: (1) the research questions being addressed are "how" or "why" questions, (2) little control exists over events, and (3) the focus is on a contemporary, real-life phenomenon in which context is important (Yin, 1994).

CASE SELECTION CRITERIA

This book is based on six of the twenty-six institutions that participated in the ACE Project on Leadership and Institutional Transformation, a five-and-a-half-year initiative on institutional transformation funded by the W. K. Kellogg Foundation. The data reported were collected and analyzed as part of the work of the Kellogg Forum on Higher Education Transformation. Qualitative research techniques were used, including interviews, participant observation, site visits, and document analysis.

Twenty-six institutions were selected to participate in the ACE project through a national competition from a pool of 110 applicants. Selection of the original group of institutions was based on the following criteria: (1) the proposed change altered more than the structure of the institution and touched core values, underlying assumptions, behaviors, processes, and products; (2) the proposed change was deep and pervasive, impacting much if not all of the campus; (3) the change was intentional—there was clear articulation of the proposed change and what the institution sought to accomplish; (4) the change was intended to be long-term; and (5) the campus would create structures (or already had them in place) to engage faculty in leading change. Having a variety of institutional types that reflected the rich diversity of American higher education was also important.

Because the intent of the project was to not only follow and learn from the experiences of participating institutions but also assist their progress on their transformational agendas, we made sure that the original twenty-six institutions included a mix of colleges and universities (1) that were just embarking on change, (2) that had recently begun but made little progress, and (3) that had strong track records of change. Thus, we also purposefully attempted to include multiple types of institutions in our selection (Yin, 1985).

A subset of six institutions that made the most progress toward transformation was identified for this study from the twenty-three ACE institutions that elected to continue into year 4 of the project. The following criteria were used to determine which institutions were making the most progress toward transformational change: (1) they met institutionally defined goals; (2) they illustrated change in values, underlying assumptions, behaviors, processes, products, and structure; (3) they provided evidence of a change in institutional culture; and (4) they demonstrated mechanisms of sustainability, such as new positions or divisions, changed policies and strategic directions, and the commitment and investment of resources. Although the initial twenty-three institutions originally intended to make transformational change, only the subset of six met these criteria and could be labeled as transforming institutions. These distinctive institutions provided important data for understanding what processes help promote transformation since all institutions had a clear intent to effect transformation and the support of the ACE project, but all did not make equal progress toward their goals.

The researchers identified the six institutions as having made the most progress by reviewing the documentation provided by the institutions, by visiting institutions, and by soliciting the opinions of ACE consultants and staff who had conducted the campus visits and provided consultation to campuses. Following the lead of Birnbaum (1992), who in his longitudinal leadership study notes the long tradition of this qualitative approach, we asked campus visitors to provide their judgments of progress in global, comprehensive terms and to determine the extent to which the institutions were "significantly changed" at the end of five years. We asked the visitors to describe the ways in which the campuses were different, which gave us a set of comparative indicators that we outlined in the second chapter. The six transforming institutions represented a range of organizational complexity, from a small liberal arts college with seventy-two faculty to a four-campus community college serving more than fifty thousand students.

DATA COLLECTION AND ANALYSIS

This section describes the data collection and analysis strategies used in the project. It describes the relationship between project staff and campus leaders, the visits, and the project reports writing. The second part of this section describes the data analysis techniques.

Primary Informants

At all institutions in the ACE project, a primary informant—someone who would be centrally involved in all aspects of managing the change process and could arrange access to key people and documents (Merriam,

1988)—was identified by the chief academic officer (CAO). The primary informant was the key leader of the institution's efforts with change, a project chair. The project chair tended to be one of three people: the CAO, a different senior administrator, or a senior faculty member. At a few institutions, two people acted as co-informants as their efforts were led by co-chairs. This person acted as the primary conduit throughout the project. In all cases the original project chair remained the same over the course of the project.

We contacted the project chair early in the project to review the objectives of the project, describe the various strategies to collect data, discuss the intended outcomes of the campus initiative, and gain a commitment to participate in ways consistent with the project structure.

Preparation of Research Team

The research teams consisted of ACE staff and external consultants working on the project who were seasoned senior administrators, and experienced higher education management consultants (three of the four were former college presidents). Project staff—ACE staff and consultants—met twice prior to the launch of the project to review project goals and assumptions, discuss site visit protocols and data collection procedures, and review initial documentation sent by the participating institutions and their project applications. Project staff read and discussed common readings and additional materials produced by ACE to frame the efforts and provide a common conceptual framework for transformation, discussed the project's intent and objectives, and reviewed site visit protocols and data collection procedures. Consultants refined the procedures through meetings and discussions and sharpened the visit protocols and framing questions to be used in the project.

Project staff continued to meet every six months for two days to debrief from their campus visits and phone conversations. Additional, periodic conference calls were held among project staff to supplement the face-to-face meetings.

Visit Process

In the first three years, two site visits were made each year; in the last two years, one visit occurred annually. In addition to site visits, eight project meetings were held that brought together project staff (researchers) and institutional informants, following the same pattern as the visits. Summaries were developed from each project meeting and are another form of data. Site visits and project meetings were supplemented by participant observation, reports, and document analysis. In total, over the life of the project each institution and project staff interacted twenty-four times.

In terms of the site visit process, researchers contacted the project chair to schedule and organize each visit. In each case the lead researcher placed an initial phone call to frame the purposes and anticipated outcomes for the visit, to gain a brief understanding of the key issues on campus at that time, to work with the team chair to identify people to meet with during the visit, and to learn of the project leader's anticipated outcomes from the visit. The researcher also asked that relevant documentation be sent prior to the visit.

The researcher made a second phone call was to the project chair to review the proposed visit schedule. During this call, the researcher and project chair discussed the agenda and individuals scheduled for meetings and focus groups. The researchers in many instances asked that key people not appearing on the original list be added.

Although the nuances of the visits varied to fit local situations, they shared some common traits. Each visit lasted approximately two days. The researchers met first with the project chair to get an overview of the change efforts and the strategies being used. This private meeting also allowed the project chair to share frustrations and failures with the researchers. The visits tended to conclude with a private meeting with the president and/or CAO. This structure allowed the researchers to discuss difficult matters confidentially and to provide an initial debriefing of the visit with senior leaders as a way to test early assumptions and insights. The other visit meetings and focus groups varied from campus to campus. However, each visit included substantial time with the campus leadership team responsible for shepherding the changes, focus groups with faculty directly involved in leading the change efforts as well as faculty who were affected by the emerging changes. In some instances, administrators from other areas such as student affairs, business affairs, government relations, development, and admissions participated in focus groups. At other times, researchers conducted focus groups with the administrative cabinet, the institution's vice presidents and senior administrators reporting to the president. In some instances, researchers met with students. The focus groups ranged from three people to twelve. In a few instances more participated. Researchers worked to keep the groups smaller than ten, but not always successfully. Most focus groups tended to last between sixty and ninety minutes. However, some conversations with key administrators or faculty leaders were longer.

After the visits, researchers independently wrote up their notes. From these working documents, the lead researcher crafted two reports. The first report was to the campus project leader summarizing the visit. The second report, following an established template, was to ACE staff that described the change process, the areas of success and failure, and the contextual nuances of the change at that specific campus. We drew upon both sets of documents in the analysis. Triangulation of data was achieved through multiple site visit observers and interviewees as well as observation from primary informants and reports, which will be discussed in the next section.

Participant Observation and Reports

On each campus, researchers worked with the primary informant to collect information to supplement the visits. The primary informant was asked to keep a record that would be used to develop written reports. Guidance was given for how to document events, challenges, and successes. The primary informants provided reports to ACE twice a year for the first two years and once a year for the last two years. Each of the written reports produced by each primary informant followed a common template and addressed specific questions regarding the process of change. The reports were confidential to ACE staff, allowing informants to write with less constraint than if the reports were shared among project institutions. Frequently, reports were sent back to the primary informant by the researcher for additional information. In some instances, supplemental public reports were written, mostly at the request of other project institutions. Participants also provided researchers with related documents prior to each visit and meeting. Researchers also collected key documents during their visits. The documents collected, while varying among institutions, included the following: campus newspaper articles, memorandum, survey results, speeches, foundation proposals, strategic plans, white papers, retreat agendas and summaries, meeting minutes, and annual reports.

Data Analysis

We used qualitative research techniques including interviews, participant observation, site visits, and document analysis to understand transformational change. A project team of ACE staff and senior consultants worked closely with and observed the change process at the twenty-three project institutions. Over the life of the project, each institution and the researchers interacted twenty-four times. A project consultant—who was a former college president or experienced higher education management consultant—or an ACE staff member visited each campus twice a year during the first three years. During the last two years, a two-person team of project consultants and ACE staff who had not been affiliated with that particular institution during the first phase visited each campus once. For the first three years, ACE held two project meetings a year for leadership teams of faculty and administrators and requested two written self-evaluations each year. During the final two years, ACE convened institutional project teams annually and requested a written report prior to each meeting.

For each institution, the researchers created a case portfolio of all sources of data. Within the portfolio were the institution's application for the project, eight written reports from the institution, eight campus visit reports by project staff, notes from phone conversations, summaries of project meeting discussions, and other documents produced by the institution relating to the transformation effort.

Data analysis was conducted using three different approaches: (1) categorical analysis, (2) memoing, and (3) narrative analysis. Categorical analysis was used to identify change strategies, beginning with those described in literature review (Miles & Huberman, 1994). Emergent themes were identified and negotiated between the two reviewers. An example of a theme that emerged was the notion of balance. Both reviewers identified this theme independently; then analyses of the theme were compared. Themes were often discussed with the site visit teams or members of the campuses for further elaboration and exploration. Second, memoing, a process of writing up ideas of the pattern coded data, helped to identify interrelationship among themes (Miles & Huberman, 1994).

Finally, the themes were illuminated through narrative analysis. Stories of change were developed from the rich data collected throughout the project. The data presented in this book are modified versions of the narratives that were developed. The narratives integrate disparate data into a whole, more accurately representing how change occurs (rather than listing separate unrelated processes). The researchers took care not to force relationships. This analysis technique helped illustrate the contextual issues critical to change and the interrelatedness of the identified themes (Reissman, 1993).

After the analysis was completed, various components of the findings were shared and discussed with representatives from campuses and with ACE staff and project consultants to confirm our interpretations, refine our insights, and avoid researcher bias.

RIGOR AND LIMITATIONS

To ensure rigor, the researchers followed qualitative research strategies outlined by Yin (1994). We used multiple sources of evidence to create "converging lines of inquiry." We constructed a database of information for each case and developed a logical chain of evidence that linked the analysis to specific instances in the case database and to the research questions. To ensure trustworthiness, the researchers independently reviewed the data and drew conclusions, engaged in peer debriefing, and used a participant check (Lincoln & Guba, 1985).

Nonetheless, this research is not without limitations. First, the original intent of the project was not to conduct experimental research but to assist institutions to develop their capacity for reflection and change. Institutions were not selected in the ACE project for their representativeness but rather for the likelihood of making progress. Second, because institutions self-selected to be part of the larger project from which this subsample was taken, they may not represent the range of institutions undergoing transformational change. Third, because much of the data is self-reported, it may be biased to reflect success. Fourth, institutional transformation journeys for the most part are continuing after the five years of the project, making it difficult to determine the success of the change initiatives as they go on today or have changed over time to reflect new environmental challenges and conditions. Fifth, participation in the national project most likely had some effect on the institutions in the study. Because it sought to help campuses make progress toward goals, the project consisted of interventions that may have facilitated the transformation process, particularly national project meetings, campus site visits, and report writing, all of which asked people to reflect on the change process and provided external encouragement.

Bibliography

Adelman, Clifford. (2000). *A parallel postsecondary universe: The certification system in information technology*. Washington, DC: Office of Educational Research and Improvement (ED).

Alpert, Daniel. (1991). Performance and paralysis: The organizational context of the American research university. In Marvin Peterson, Ellen E. Chaffee, and Theodore H. White (Eds.), *Organization and governance in higher education* (4th ed.) (pp. 76–102). Needham Heights, MA: Ginn Press.

Argyris, Chris. (1994). *On organizational learning* (2nd ed.). Cambridge, MA: Blackwell.

Bartunek, Jane M. (1984). Changing interpretive schemes and organizational restructuring: The example of a religious order. *Administrative Science Quarterly, 29*, 355–372.

Bensimon, Estella, and Anna Neumann. (1993). *Redesigning collegiate leadership*. Baltimore: John Hopkins University Press.

Bergquist, William H. (1992). *The four cultures of the academy: Insights and strategies for improving leadership in collegiate organizations*. San Francisco: Jossey-Bass.

Birnbaum, Robert. (1988). *How colleges work: The cybernetics of academic organization and leadership*. San Francisco: Jossey-Bass.

Birnbaum, Robert. (1992). *How academic leadership works: Understanding success and failure in the college presidency*. San Francisco: Jossey-Bass.

Birnbaum, Robert. (2000). *Management fads in higher education: Where they come from, what they do, why they fail*. San Francisco: Jossey-Bass.

Boeker, Warren. (1997). Strategic change: The influence of managerial characteristics and organizational growth. *Academy of Management Journal, 40*, 152–169.

Bolman, Lee. G., and Terrance E. Deal. (1991). *Reframing organizations: Artistry, choice and leadership*. San Francisco: Jossey-Bass.

Boyer, Ernest L. (1990). *Scholarship reconsidered: Priorities of the professoriate*. Princeton, NJ: The Carnegie Foundation for the Advancement of Teaching.

Brimah, Tunde. (2000.) *Roster of for-profit educational institutions*. Education Commission of the States. www. ecs.org.

Burns, T., and G. M. Stalker. (1961). *The management of innovation*. London: Tavistock.

Cameron, Kim. (1991). Organizational adaptation and higher education. In Marvin Peterson, Ellen E. Chaffee, and Theodore H. White (Eds.), *Organization and governance in higher education* (4th ed.) (pp. 284–299). Needham Heights, MA: Ginn Press.

Carnevale, Anthony P., and Richard A. Fry. (2001). *Crossing the great divide*. Washington, DC: Educational Testing Services.

Chaffee, Ellen E. (1991). Three models of strategy. In Marvin Peterson, Ellen E. Chaffee, and Theodore H. White (Eds.), *ASHE reader on organization and governance in higher education* (pp. 225–238). Needham Heights, MA: Ginn Press.

Chaffee, Ellen E., and William G. Tierney. (1988). *Collegiate culture and leadership strategies*. American Council on Education/Macmillan Series on Higher Education. Washington, DC: American Council on Education.

Clark, Burton, R. (1995). Complexity and differentiation: The deepening problem of university integration. In David D. Dill and Barbara Sporn (Eds.), *Emerging patterns of social demand and university reform: Through a glass darkly* (pp. 159–170). Tarrytown, NY: IAU Press.

Clark, Burton, R. (1998). *Creating entrepreneurial universities: Organizational pathways of transformation*. New York: International Association of Universities Press.

Cohen, Michael D., and James G. March. (1986). *Leadership and ambiguity* (2nd ed.). Boston: Harvard Business School Press.

Cowan, Ruth. B. (1993). Prescription for small-college turnaround. *Change, 25*(1), 30–39.

Curry, Barbara. (1992). Instituting enduring innovations: Achieving continuity of change in higher education. *ASHE-ERIC Higher Education Report Series*. Washington, DC: George Washington University.

Duderstadt, James J. (2000). *University for the 21st Century*. Ann Arbor: University of Michigan Press.

Eccles, Robert G., and Nitin Nohria. (1992). *Beyond the hype: Rediscovering the essence of management*. Boston: Harvard Business School Press.

Eckel, Peter D. (1998). *How institutions discontinue academic programs: Making potentially adverse decisions in an environment of shared decision-making*. Unpublished doctoral dissertation, University of Maryland, College Park.

Eckel, Peter D., Barbara Hill, and Madeleine Green. (1998). *En route to transformation* (On Change Occasional Paper No. 1). Washington, DC: American Council on Education.

Eckel, Peter D., Madeleine Green, and Barbara Hill. (2001). *Riding the waves of change* (On Change Occasional Paper No. 5). Washington, DC: American Council on Education.

Eckel, Peter D., Barbara Hill, Madeleine Green, and Bill Mallon. (1999). *Taking charge of change: A primer for colleges and universities*. (On Change Occasional Paper No. 3). Washington, DC: American Council on Education.

El-Khawas, Elaine. (1995). External review: Alternative models based on US experience. *Higher Education Management, 7*(1), 39–48.

Fisher, James L., Marsha Tack, and Karen Wheeler. (1988). *The effective college president*. New York: ACE/Macmillan.

Gardenswartz, Lee, and Anita Rowe. (1994). *Diverse teams at work: Capitalizing on power of diversity*. Chicago: Irwin.

Gioia, Dennis A., and Kumar Chittipeddi. (1991). Sensemaking and sensegiving in strategic change initiation. *Strategic Management Journal, 12,* 433–448.

Gioia, Dennis A., and James B. Thomas. (1996). Identity, image, and issue interpretation: Sensemaking during strategic change in academia. *Administrative Science Quarterly, 41,* 370–403.

Gioia, Dennis A., James B. Thomas, Shawn M. Clark, and Kumar Chittipeddi. (1996). Symbolism and strategic change in academia: The dynamics of sensemaking and influence. In James R. Meindl, Charles Stubbart, Joseph F. Porac (Eds.), *Cognition within and between organization* (pp. 207–244). Thousand Oaks, CA: Sage.

Green, Madeleine, and Fred Hayward. (1997). Forces for change. In Madeleine F. Green (Ed.), *Transforming higher education* (pp. 3–26). Washington, DC: American Council on Education.

Green, Madeleine, Peter Eckel, and Andris Barblan. (2002). *The brave new (and smaller) world of higher education: A transatlantic view*. (The Changing Enterprise Occasional Paper No. 1.) Washington, DC: American Council on Education.

Gumport, Patricia J. (1993). Contested terrain of academic program reduction. *Journal of Higher Education, 64*(3), 283–311.

Gumport, Patricia J., and Barbara Sporn. (1999). Institutional adaptation: Demands for management reform and university administration. In J. Smart (Ed.), *Higher education: Handbook of theory and research, Vol. 14*. New York: Agathon.

Guskin, Alan E. (1994). *Reducing student costs and enhancing student learning* (AGB Occasional Papers No. 27). Washington, DC: Association of Governing Boards of Universities and Colleges.

Guskin, Alan E. (1996). Facing the future: The change process in restructuring universities. *Change, 28*(4), 27–37.

Hardy, Cynthia, Ann Langley, Henry Mintzberg, and Janet Rose. (1983). Strategy formation in the university setting. *Review of Higher Education, 4,* 407–433.

Harvey, William. (2001). *Minorities in higher education 2000–2001: Eighteenth annual status report*. Washington, DC: American Council on Education.

Hayward, Fred. (2000). *Internationalization of U.S. higher education: Preliminary status report, 2000*. Washington, DC: American Council on Education.

Hearn, James C. (1996). Transforming U.S. higher education: An organizational perspective. *Innovative Higher Education, 21*, 141–154.

Heifetz, Ronald A. (1994). *Leadership without easy answers*. Cambridge, MA: Harvard University Press.

Hodgkinson, Harold L. (1999). *All one system: A second look*. Washington, DC: Institute for Educational Leadership and The National Center for Public Policy and Higher Education.

Hovey, Harold A. (1999). *State spending for higher education in the next decade: The battle to sustain current support*. San Jose, CA: National Center for Public Policy and Higher Education, State Policy Research.

Ikenberry, Stanley O., and Terry W. Hartle. (2000). *Taking stock: How Americans judge, quality, affordability, and leadership at U.S. colleges and universities*. Washington, DC: American Council on Education.

Kaiser, James R., and Paula R. Kaiser. (1994). Persuasive messages to support planned change. *College and University, 69*(2), 124–129.

Katz, Richard N. (1999). *Dancing with the devil: Information technology and the new competition in higher education*. San Francisco: Jossey-Bass.

Kerr, Clark. (1984). *Presidents make a difference: Strengthening leadership in colleges and universities*. Washington, DC: Association of Governing Boards of Universities and Colleges.

Kerr, Clark, and Marian Gade. (1986). *The many lives of academic presidents*. Washington, DC: Association of Governing Boards of Universities and Colleges.

Kezar, Adrianna J. (2001). *Understanding and facilitating organizational change in the 21st century* (ASHE-ERIC Higher Education Report, 28[4]). San Francisco: Jossey-Bass.

Kezar, Adrianna, and Peter Eckel. (2002). The effect of institutional culture on change strategies in higher education: Universal principles or culturally responsive concepts? *Journal of Higher Education, 73*, 435–460.

King, Jacqueline. (1999). *Money matters: The impact of race/ethnicity and gender on how students pay for college*. Washington, DC: American Council on Education.

Klein, Katherine J., and Joanne Speer Sorra. (1996). The challenge of innovation implementation. *Academy of Management Review, 21*, 1055–1808.

Kriger, Thomas J. (2001). *A virtual revolution: Trends in the expansion of distance education*. Washington, DC: American Federation of Teachers.

Kuh, George D., and Elizabeth J. Whitt. (1988). *The invisible tapestry: Culture in American colleges and universities* (ASHE-ERIC Higher Education Report No. 1). Washington, DC: Association for the Study of Higher Education.

Leifer, Richard, Gina C. O'Connor, and Mark Rice. (2001). Implementing radical innovation in mature firms: The role of hubs. *Academy of Management Executive, 15*(3), 102–113.

Leslie, David, and E. K. Fretwell. (1996). *Wise moves in hard times*. San Francisco: Jossey-Bass.

Levine, Arthur. (1980). *Why innovation fails: The institutionalization and termination of innovation in higher education*. Albany: State University of New York Press.

Lincoln, Yvonne S., and Egon G. Guba. (1985). *Naturalistic inquiry*. Beverly Hills, CA: Sage.

Lindquist, Jack. (1978). *Strategies for change*. Berkeley, CA: Pacific Soundings.

Lovett, Clara. (1993). To affect intimately the lives of the people: American professors and their society. *Change*, 25(4), 26–37.

Maassen, Peter, Guy Neave, and Ben Jongbloed. (1999). Organizational adaptation in higher education. In Ben Jongbloed, Peter Massen, and Guy Neave (Eds.), *From the eye of the storm: Higher education's changing institution*. Boston: Kluwer Academic.

March, James G. (1994). *A primer on decision making: How decisions happen*. New York: Free Press.

Marginson, Simon, and Mark Considine. (2000). *The enterprise university: Power, governance, and reinvention in Australia*. New York: Cambridge University Press.

McMahon, Joan, and Robert Caret. (1997). Redesigning the faculty roles and rewards structure. *Metropolitan Universities*, 7(4), 11–22.

Meister, Jeanne C. (2001, February 9). The brave new world of corporate education. *Chronicle of Higher Education*, p. B10.

Miles, Matthew B., and A. Michael Huberman. (1994). *Qualitative data analysis* (2nd ed.). Thousand Oaks, CA: Sage.

Millar, Susan, and Alan Roberts. (1993). *Monological innovation versus polylogical improvement*. State College: Pennsylvania State University.

Mintzberg, Henry. (1983). *Structures in fives: Designing effective organizations*. Englewood Cliffs, NJ: Prentice Hall.

Mintzberg, Henry. (1987, July–August). Crafting strategy. *Harvard Business Review*, pp. 66–75.

Mintzberg, Henry. (1994). *The rise and fall of strategic planning*. New York: Free Press.

Mone, Mark A., William McKinley, and Vincent L. Barker, III. (1998). Organizational decline and innovation: A contingency framework. *Academy of Management Review*, 23, 115–132.

Morgan, Gareth. (1986). *Images of organizations*. Newbury Park, CA: Sage.

Morino Institute. (2001). *Venture philanthropy: The changing landscape*. Washington, DC: Morino Institute.

Newman, Adam E., Yegin Chen, and Sean Gallagher. (2002, January). Charting the course: E-learning providers respond to market conditions. (As summarized in *The Forecast*.) *University Business*, pp. 25–32.

Newman, Frank, and Lara Couturier. (2001). *The new competitive arena: Market forces invade the academy*. The Futures Project. Providence, RI: Brown University.

Newman, Frank, and Jamie Scurry. (2001). *Higher education in the digital rapids*. The Futures Project. Providence, RI: Brown University.

Obligner, Dianne G., Carole A. Barone, and Brian L. Hawkins. (2001). *Distributed education: Challenges, choices, and a new environment*. Washington, DC: American Council on Education.

O'Neill, Hugh M., Richard W. Pouder, and Anne, K. Buchholtz. (1998). Patterns in the diffusion of strategies across organizations: Insights from the innovation diffusion literature. *Academy of Management Review, 23*, 98–114.

Peterson, Marvin, and Melinda G. Spencer. (1991). Understanding academic culture and climate. In Marvin W. Peterson, Ellen E. Chaffee, and Theodore H. White (Eds.), *ASHE Reader on Organization and Governance* (pp. 140–155). Needham Heights, MA: Simon and Schuster.

Pettigrew, Andrew M. (1995). Longitudinal field research on change: Theory and practice. In G. P. Huber and A. H. Van de Ven (Eds.), *Longitudinal field research methods: Studying processes of organizational change* (pp. 91–125). Thousand Oaks, CA: Sage.

Presley, Jennifer B., and David W. Leslie. (1999). Understanding strategy: An assessment of theory and practice. In John C. Smart and William G. Tierney (Eds.), *Higher education: Handbook of theory and research, Vol. 14* (pp. 201–239). New York: Agathon Press.

Rajagopalan, Nandini, and Gretchen M. Spreitzer. (1996). Toward a theory of strategic change: A multi-lens perspective and integrative framework. *Academy of Management Review, 22*, 48–79.

Ramaley, Judith. (1995). *Report on assessment and accountability*. Portland, OR: Portland State University.

Reissman, Catherine. (1993). *Narrative analysis*. Beverly Hills: Sage.

Roberts, Alton O., Jon F. Wergin, and Bronwyn E. Adam. (1993). Institutional approaches to the issues of reward and scholarship. *New Directions for Higher Education*, no. 81, 63–86.

Rogers, Everett M. (1962). *Diffusion of innovations*. New York: Free Press of Glencoe.

Salipante, Paul F., and Karen Golden-Biddle. (1995). Managing traditionality and strategic change in non-profit organizations. *Non-Profit Management and Leadership, 6*, 3–20.

Schein, Edgar H. (1992). *Organizational culture and leadership* (2nd ed.). San Francisco: Jossey-Bass.

Schon, Donald A. (1983). *The reflective practitioner: How professionals think in action*. New York: Basic Books.

Senge, Peter M. (1992). *The fifth discipline: The art and practice of the learning organization*. New York: Doubleday.

Smircich, Linda. (1983). Organizations as shared meanings. In Louis R. Pondy, Peter J. Frost, Gareth Morgan, and Thomas C. Dandridge (Eds.), *Organizational symbolism* (pp. 55–65). Greenwich, CT: JAI.

Sporn, Barbara. (1999). *Adaptive university structures: An analysis of adaptation to socioeconomic environments of US and European universities.* Philadelphia: Francis and Taylor, Higher Education Policy Series 54; London: Jessica Kingsley.

Stake, R. E. (1995). *The art of case study research.* Thousand Oaks, CA: Sage.

Starbuck, William H., and Francis J. Milliken. (1988). Executives' perceptual filters: What they notice and how they make sense. In Donald C. Hambrick (Ed.), *The executive effect: Concepts and methods for studying top managers* (pp. 35–65). Greenwich, CT: JAI.

St. John, Edward P. (1991). The transformation of private liberal arts colleges. *Review of Higher Education, 15*(1), 83–106.

Sutcliffe, Kathleen M. (1994). What executives notice: Accurate perceptions in top management teams. *Academy of Management Journal, 37,* 1360–1378.

Taylor, Alton, and Audrey M. Koch. (1996). The cultural context for effective strategy. *New Directions for Higher Education,* no. 94, 83–86.

Tierney, William G. (1991). Academic work and institutional culture: Constructing knowledge. *Review of Higher Education, 14*(2), 199–216.

Tierney, William G., and Robert Rhoads. (1993). *Enhancing promotion, tenure, and beyond: Faculty socialization as a cultural process.* Washington, DC: ASHE-ERIC Higher Education Reports.

Twigg, Carol A. (1999). *Improving learning and reducing costs: Redesigning large-enrollment courses.* Philadelphia: Pew Charitable Trusts.

Walker, Donald E. (1979). *The effective administrator.* San Francisco: Jossey-Bass.

Weick, Karl E. (1983). Educational organizations as loosely coupled systems. In J. Victor Baldridge and Terrance Deal (Eds.), *The dynamics of organizational change in education* (pp. 15–37). Berkeley, CA: McCutchan.

Weick. Karl E. (1995). *Sensemaking in organizations.* Thousand Oaks, CA: Sage.

Wheatley, Margaret J. (1994). *Leadership and the new science: Discovering order in a chaotic world* (2nd ed.). San Francisco: Berrett-Koehler.

White, Geoffry D., and Flannery C. Hauck. (2000). *Campus, inc. Corporate power in the ivory tower.* Amherst, NY: Prometheus Books.

Yin, Robert K. (1994). *Case study research: Design and methods.* Thousand Oaks, CA: Sage.

Index

About the Authors

PETER D. ECKEL Ph.D. is the Associate Director for Institutional Initiatives at the American Council on Education (ACE) where he works primarily with initiatives related to institutional change. He directs the Changing Enterprises Project, a two-year effort to explore the new ways in which institutions are responding to a changing competitive and technologically-rich environment through strategic alliances. His articles have appeared in *The Review of Higher Education, Planning for Higher Education, The Journal of Higher Education, Metropolitan Universities Journal, To Improve the Academy, Research in Higher Education*, and *Higher Education Policy*. He has been a fellow at the Salzburg Seminar Universities Project in Austria and at the Centre for Higher Education Transformation (CHET) in South Africa. In 1998, he received his Ph.D. in education policy, planning, and administration from the University of Maryland, College Park.

ADRIANNA KEZAR Ph.D. is assistant professor at the University of Maryland, College Park, in the Higher Education Administration Program. She has over forty published articles, books, and chapters on the topics of leadership, governance, and change and innovation. Her work has been featured in top tiered education journals including *The Journal of Higher Education, The Review of Higher Education*, and *Research in Higher Education*. Her latest book is entitled, *Understanding and Facilitating Organizational Change in the 21st Century* (2001). Kezar has developed a national leadership conference for administrators and faculty in higher education based on her research. She previously served as director of the ERIC Clearinghouse for Higher Education and currently is managing editor of the ASHE-ERIC higher education report series. She received her Ph.D. in education from the University of Michigan.